THE
AWESOME
BOOK
OF
BiBLE
ANSWERS
FOR KIDS!

THE
AWESOME
BOOK
OF BIBLE
ANSWERS
FOR KIDS!

JOSH McDOWELL
KEVIN JOHNSON

HARVEST HOUSE PUBLISHERS

EUGENE, OREGON

Cover by Koechel Peterson & Associates, Inc., Minneapolis, Minnesota

Interior illustrations © Kreig Barrie

THE AWESOME BOOK OF BIBLE ANSWERS FOR KIDS
Copyright © 2003 by Josh McDowell and Kevin Johnson
Published by Harvest House Publishers
Eugene, Oregon 97402
www.harvesthousepublishers.com

Library of Congress Cataloging-in-Publication Data
McDowell, Josh.
    [Children demand a verdict]
    The awesome book of Bible answers for kids / Josh McDowell and Kevin Johnson.
       p. cm.
    Originally published: Children demand a verdict. Wheaton, Ill. : Tyndale House Publishers, ©2003.
    Includes indexes.
    ISBN 978-0-7369-2872-4 (pbk.)
    1. Apologetics. 2. Christianity—Miscellanea. I. Johnson, Kevin (Kevin Walter) II. Title.
    BT1103.M325 2011
    239—dc22

                          2010021675

Printed in the United States of America

        11 12 13 14 15 16 17 18 19 / VP-SK / 10 9 8 7 6 5 4 3 2 1

The word of the LORD holds true,
and everything he does is worthy of our trust.
He loves whatever is just and good,
and his unfailing love fills the earth.

PSALM 33:4-5

Contents

That's a good question! 13

QUESTIONS ABOUT GOD

1. Why did God make people? 17

2. How do we know what God is like
when we can't see him? 18

QUESTIONS ABOUT SIN

3. Why do I feel bad when I do something wrong? 21

4. What if I don't feel bad when I do
something wrong? 22

5. Why does sin keep me from being friends
with God? 23

6. Why does God say the punishment for
sin is death? 24

7. Why doesn't God just forget our sins? 25

8. Are "little" sins okay with God? 26

9. Why is sin sometimes fun? 27

QUESTIONS ABOUT FORGIVENESS

10. Why did Jesus die? 31

11. Why did Jesus have to die for my sin
when I haven't done anything really bad? 32

12. Will God forgive really bad people? 33

13. Does God always forgive me? 34

QUESTIONS ABOUT GOD'S LOVE

14. How do I know God wants to be my friend? 37

15. What kind of friend is God? 38

16. Does God love me more when I obey him? 39

17. How can I be better friends with God? 40

18. How much does God love me? 41

19. How can God have time for me when there
are so many other people in the world? 42

20. Will God ever stop loving me? 43

21. Does God like my sister more than me? 44

QUESTIONS ABOUT PRAYER

22. Is God ever too busy to listen to my prayers? 47

23. Is God really interested in my problems? 48

24. Will God give me whatever I ask for when I pray? 49

QUESTIONS ABOUT JESUS

25. Did Jesus ever do anything wrong? 53

26. Was Jesus ever tempted to sin? 54

27. How can Jesus live inside me? 55

28. Was Jesus a wimp? 56

29. Did Jesus know he was God? 57

30. Did everyone in the Bible think Jesus was God? 58

31. Did Jesus actually die on the cross—
or did he just faint? 59

32. Did Jesus really come back to life after he
died on the cross? 60

33. Could Jesus' disciples have made up the story
about Jesus coming back to life? 61

34. How did Jesus come back to life? 62

35. Is it okay to have Easter baskets
and look for Easter eggs? 63

QUESTIONS ABOUT THE HOLY SPIRIT

36. What's the Holy Spirit? Is he a ghost? 67

37. How come I can't feel the Holy Spirit living in me? 68

QUESTION ABOUT THE DEVIL

38. Is the devil real? 71

QUESTIONS ABOUT THE BIBLE

39. How do some people know so much about God? 75

40. Why is the Bible so big? 76

41. How is the Bible different from other books? 77

42. Why did God put his words in a book? 78

43. How could God write a book? 79

44. Who wrote down the words in the Bible? 80

45. How do we know the Bible is from God? 81

46. The Bible is so old. How could it last so long? 82

47. Are parts of the Bible make-believe,
or is everything true? 83

48. What will happen to people who don't
obey the Bible? 84

49. Why is the Bible so hard to understand? 85

50. Why does the Bible have so many rules? 86

51. Are the Bible's rules old-fashioned? 87

52. Is the Bible always right? 88

53. Why are there so many different kinds of Bibles? 89

QUESTIONS ABOUT DIFFERENT RELIGIONS

54. Why do people from different religions
sometimes fight? 93

55. Does my Muslim friend pray to the same God I do? . . . 94

56. Do I have to tell people about Jesus? 95

57. Does it matter which God people believe in? 96

QUESTIONS ABOUT RIGHT AND WRONG

58. Can I decide for myself what's right and wrong? 99

59. Why do we need rules? 100

60. Does God punish me when I do wrong? 101

61. Why is it sometimes easier to do things that
are wrong than to do what's right? 102

62. How does God help me choose to do the right thing? 103

63. Why do I sometimes get in trouble for doing
the right thing? 104

64. Why do some Christians not act like Christians? 105

QUESTIONS ABOUT THE FUTURE

65. Does God know what my life will be
like when I grow up? 109

66. Does God care what job I have when I grow up? 110

67. Will God tell me what will happen in my future? 111

68. Why does God let bad things happen
to me sometimes? 112

69. Can God make bad things turn out okay? 113

QUESTIONS ABOUT CHURCH

70. Why do we go to church? 117

71. Why does church last so long? 118

72. My friend doesn't go to church—
what should I do? 119

QUESTIONS ABOUT DEATH AND HEAVEN

73. Why did my grandma die when the Bible
says that Christians will live forever? 123

74. What will I look like in heaven? 124

75. Will everybody go to heaven? 125

76. How long will we be in heaven? 126

77. How do I know I'm going to heaven? 127

Learning and conversation guide for parents 129

Index of Bible verses 151

Index of topics by question number 153

That's a good question!

You probably wonder about Jesus and God sometimes. Maybe you want to know why the Bible is such a big deal—or have other questions.

These kinds of questions are great—because what you know and believe about God, Jesus, and the Bible makes a big difference to who you are deep down inside. So keep reading, and keep asking those great questions!

Mom and Dad and other grown-ups—you'll want to take a look at page 129, where the Learning and Conversation Guide starts. You'll find good ideas to illustrate the answers in this book, and tips on how to talk about the faith and live it out.

QUESTIONS ABOUT GOD

1. Why did God make people?

God made us to be his friends. When God made the sun and the moon, the land and the sea, and the plants and animals that fill our world, he was pleased. But when he made people, he said that we were an extra-special creation. Why? Because he made us so that we're able to know him! We can talk to him and read about him. From the beginning of the Bible to the end, there's a clear message: God loves us, and he wants us to love him back. He wants us to trust him, enjoy him, and obey him. His plan is for us to live every minute as his friends. And someday he wants us to live with him in heaven forever!

> God looked over all he had made, and he
> saw that it was excellent in every way.
>
> **GENESIS 1:31**

2. How do we know what God is like when we can't see him?

We can't see God, because God is a spirit. He doesn't have a physical body like we do. God knew that it would be hard for us to understand exactly what he is like. So he came up with a wonderful way for us to know him. God, the Father, sent his Son, Jesus, to be born as a baby in Bethlehem. Jesus grew up and lived as a man—a very special, kind, perfect man. We can be sure that when we learn what Jesus is like, we will know what God is like. Jesus is just like God, his Father in heaven. In fact, Jesus *is* God! Jesus shows us exactly what God is like!

No one has ever seen God. But his only Son, who is himself God, is near to the Father's heart; he has told us about him.

JOHN 1:18

QUESTIONS ABOUT SIN

3. Why do I feel bad when I do something wrong?

You might *know* that you filled a bathtub with water that's too hot to climb in. But it's the way you *feel* that makes you jump out before you get burned any worse. In the same way, God planned for you to think about the way you *feel* when you have done something wrong. Doing wrong usually makes you feel far from God and from the people you hurt. Those sad feelings are a powerful message that you have done something that needs to be fixed. It's one way God helps you know you need to admit your sin to him—and do whatever you can to fix what you did wrong.

What joy for those whose record the LORD has cleared of sin, whose lives are lived in complete honesty! When I refused to confess my sin, I was weak and miserable, and I groaned all day long.

PSALM 32:2-3

4. What if I don't feel bad when I do something wrong?

Some cars come with alarm systems. They are supposed to keep people from trying to steal the car or smash it up. But it's possible to unhook an alarm so it doesn't go off. That's what it's like if you pretend you don't feel bad when you've done something wrong. God created you to have an "alarm"—to feel bad for doing wrong. He did that to warn you away from sin.

But sometimes you start to feel *good* when you do *bad*. You might punch your sister, for example, and smile about it. Or you might take a friend's cookie and feel good that you got it for free. Feelings should warn you away from sin, but feelings can also fool you. So God gave you his commands in the Bible. When you learn what the Bible says, you can always be sure about right and wrong.

> The law of the LORD is perfect, reviving the soul. The statutes of the LORD are trustworthy, making wise the simple...By them is your servant warned; in keeping them there is great reward.
>
> **PSALM 19:7,11**

5. Why does sin keep me from being friends with God?

God wants to be friends with each of us, but he is so special that he won't come near anything that's bad. So our sins make us God's enemy. The wrong things we do break God's laws, and they hurt the people God cares about. Since God only does what is right and loving and perfect, he can't be friends with people who don't want to be like him. And God, who does no wrong, can't allow sinful people to come near him. But God does want us to be friends with him. So he planned a way that he could fix the problem we have with sin. That's why he sent Jesus to Earth to die for our sins.

Your eyes are too pure to look on evil; you cannot tolerate wrong.

HABAKKUK 1:13

Does your mom or dad let you come in with really muddy shoes? Uh-uh. First the shoes have to come off. Then you can be with your family!

6. Why does God say the punishment for sin is death?

When our bodies quit working, we die. That's physical death. But there's another kind of death that is even worse. "Spiritual death" is when people are far from God forever and ever. It's the punishment people receive for their sins if they refuse to believe in Jesus.

That sounds bad—and it is. When God says that sin leads to death, it shows us that sin is truly awful. It also shows us that God's free gift of forgiveness is truly awesome. Jesus died to take our punishment for sin. All we have to do is believe that Jesus is God's Son and that he died for our sins. Then, instead of spiritual death, we get God's forgiveness and eternal life with him!

That's a lot to pay for a skateboard. But Jesus paid for our sin with his life!

> When people sin, they earn what sin pays—
> death. But God gives us a free gift—life
> forever in Christ Jesus our Lord.
>
> **ROMANS 6:23 NCV**

7. Why doesn't God just forget our sins?

God would never lie. So he would never pretend that we're doing what's right when we're really doing something wrong. He wouldn't be unfair. So he wouldn't act as if our sins aren't a problem. He would never say, "Oh, that's okay. It doesn't really matter. Let's just forget it."

Actually, there's something even better than God forgetting about our sins. It's God *forgiving* our sins! He wants to forgive us—to set us free from the punishment we deserve and to fix our broken friendship with him. The bad news is that God says there must be a huge payment for sin: death. The good news is that God sent his Son, Jesus, to pay for our sins. Jesus died for us and came back to life so that God could forgive us.

God sent Jesus to take the punishment for our sins and to satisfy God's anger against us. We are made right with God when we believe that Jesus shed his blood, sacrificing his life for us.

ROMANS 3:25

8. Are "little" sins okay with God?

Lots of people wonder if God gets angry at "little sins"—and we all have our ideas about which sins are little. We might think we can lie, gossip, or cheat without making God too mad.

Wondering if we can be just a little bit bad, however, makes us miss the loving purpose behind God's rules. God hates all sin (Habakkuk 1:13), and that should be a big enough reason for us to stay away from sin of any kind. But there's another reason: God commands you to be good for *your* own good. Jesus died not only so your sins could be forgiven but to free you from habits that hurt you

Is it okay to do something just a "little" stupid—like hitting only one of your thumbs with a hammer, not both?

and others. Being bad—even a "little" bad—keeps you a slave to sin and makes you miss out on God's very best for you!

Now you are no longer a slave but God's own child.

GALATIANS 4:7

9. Why is sin sometimes fun?

Suppose you want a bicycle. One day you spot a hot new bike leaning up against a store window. It's unlocked, with no owner in sight. So you swipe it. You ride it home. You scream, "Wheeeee!" all the way. Well, getting a bike God's way—by saving your money—would have been slow, hard, and costly. Doing wrong just made it feel fast, easy, and free. Sounds fun!

But sin doesn't stay fun forever, because people who disobey God won't escape punishment. God promises this: "Although the wicked flourish like weeds, and evildoers blossom with success, there is only eternal destruction ahead of them" (Psalm 92:7). Sin isn't as fast, easy, or free as it seems. It's not fun at all—in the long run!

> The way of the righteous is like the first gleam
> of dawn, which shines ever brighter until the
> full light of day. But the way of the wicked is
> like complete darkness. Those who follow it
> have no idea what they are stumbling over.
>
> **PROVERBS 4:18-19**

QUESTIONS ABOUT FORGIVENESS

10. Why did Jesus die?

Who could take the punishment for your sins? A friend couldn't pay for your sins, because friends sin just like you do. A parent couldn't take your place, because even the best parents do wrong too. A pet couldn't die for you, because an animal could not take the blame for a human being's sin. Only Jesus could die in your place. He is the only person who ever lived who never sinned—not even once. There was no reason for him to die. Jesus is the Son of God, and he was punished for your sins—so you could be forgiven!

He was wounded for the wrong we did; he was
crushed for the evil we did. The punishment,
which made us well was given to him, and
we are healed because of his wounds.

ISAIAH 53:5 NCV

11. Why did Jesus have to die for my sin when I haven't done anything really bad?

You might think of some sins as big and some as little. There's really no such thing. Some sins are easy to spot, like if you trip a friend. Some hurt people a lot, like if that friend falls down and chips a tooth. But all sins are wrong. God tells us that even every "little" sin is really bad. You also might think you don't sin very often, but we all do many wrong things.

Here's what's important to remember: All sins are bad enough that Jesus had to die for them. All sins—even one sin—hurt our friendship with God. Like James said, "The person who keeps all of the laws except one is as guilty as the person who has broken all of God's laws" (James 2:10). Being honest about your sins is the first step to understanding your need for God's forgiveness.

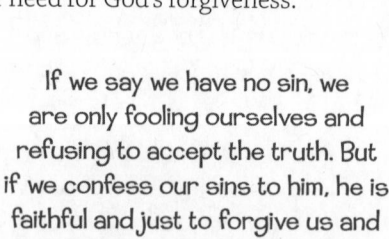

If we say we have no sin, we are only fooling ourselves and refusing to accept the truth. But if we confess our sins to him, he is faithful and just to forgive us and to cleanse us from every wrong.

1 JOHN 1:8-9

12. Will God forgive really bad people?

Jesus, God's Son, was known for hanging out with a tough crowd. He made friends with people who drank too much alcohol (Matthew 11:19). He talked with a woman people didn't like because she had been married to many husbands (John 4:1-30). He spent time with a tax collector who had cheated a lot of people (Luke 19:1-10).

So it's no surprise that God welcomes all people who admit their sin and accept his forgiveness, no matter what they have done. Jesus said that his goal is to save people who know they need his help (Mark 2:17). No matter who we are or what we have done, he wants us to remember one truth: All of us have messed up, so all of us need forgiveness.

> We are made right in God's sight when we trust in Jesus Christ to take away our sins. And we all can be saved in this same way, no matter who we are or what we have done.
>
> **ROMANS 3:22**

Q:

13. Does God always forgive me?

A:

Maybe you stay mad for a long time when a friend does something to you that's unkind or hurtful. You don't want to be friends again until you make that person as upset as you are. So you treat your friend mean until he or she says, "I'm sorry" 1000 times.

The Bible has some great news: God isn't like that! When you trust in Jesus to take away your sins, right away he makes you friends with him again. And when you ask for forgiveness, he gives it! He forgives—the first time and every time after that—whenever you need him to (1 John 1:8-9). Not only that, but God *forgets* the wrong you do. It's as if he sends your sin off to the other end of the universe, never to be seen again!

> He has taken our sins away from us as
> far as the east is from the west.
>
> **PSALM 103:12 NCV**

QUESTIONS ABOUT GOD'S LOVE

14. How do I know God wants to be my friend?

You can be sure that God is interested in being your friend because that's the whole reason why he made you. There are many places in the Bible where God calls you his sheep and tells you that you belong to him. Not only that, but God sent his Son, Jesus, to Earth because God wanted you to have a Shepherd to care for you. Jesus said, "I am the good shepherd; I know my sheep and my sheep know me—just as the Father knows me and I know the Father—and I lay down my life for the sheep" (John 10:14-15 NIV). God sent Jesus to give his life on the cross for you. God cares about you very much. In fact, he is your best Friend!

Know that the LORD is God. It is he who
made us, and we are his; we are his
people, the sheep of his pasture.

PSALM 100:3 NIV

15. What kind of friend is God?

God is a better friend than you can ever imagine. He isn't just kind—his name is love (1 John 4:7-8). He isn't just smart—he can count the hairs on your head (Matthew 10:30). He doesn't just own a big house—he rules the whole universe (Psalm 103:19).

To help you understand how great a friend God is, think of all the people you trust most. Like your parents, who give you a home, food, clothes, and love. Or your friends, who make you laugh. Or the police, who protect you. Or your favorite aunt, who never forgets your birthday. God is like all those special people rolled into one, except he is far better. He is *perfect!* No one else is as loving, powerful, kind, and smart. He is God!

LORD, you are so good,
so ready to forgive, so
full of unfailing love for
all who ask your aid...
For you are great and
perform great miracles.
You alone are God.

PSALM 86:5.10

16. Does God love me more when I obey him?

God wants you to obey him, so he is not pleased when you don't. But when you do wrong, God still loves you. In fact, he loves you just as much as if you had never sinned. God sent Jesus to die for you even before you told God you were sorry for your sin.

Now, that doesn't mean God thinks sin is okay. God feels sad when you sin. He knows that sin hurts you and the people around you. God wants you to be safe and happy, and he knows that happens only when you obey his commands. So he will help you obey when you ask him. But he will never stop loving you no matter what you do.

> God showed his great love for us by sending
> Christ to die for us while we were still sinners.
>
> **ROMANS 5:8**

17. How can I be better friends with God?

You can know *about* a famous person, but the only way you truly *know* that person is by spending time one-on-one with him or her. Your parents and pastor and Sunday school teacher can tell you all *about* God, yet what really makes you *know* him as a close friend is spending time with him for yourself.

That's what Jesus did. He took time away from his followers to talk with his heavenly Father. He went to talk to God early in the morning (Mark 1:35). And he went often (Luke 5:16). When you spend time praying to God and reading his Word, the Bible, you feel close to him all day long.

The next morning Jesus awoke long before daybreak and went out alone into the wilderness to pray.

MARK 1:35

18. How much does God love me?

Picture in your mind a sports fan who plunks down $1000 for a sweaty jersey once worn by his favorite athlete. One day that shirt will fade and tear and be tossed in the trash. But the price that fan paid tells you he is nuts about his favorite player.

Well, you have a fan who is even crazier about you. It's God! He paid a huge price to make it possible for you to become his child. He loves you so much that he sent his only Son, Jesus, from heaven to Earth. We celebrate Jesus' birth at Christmas. We thank him for dying on the cross for us on Good Friday. And we celebrate the Resurrection on Easter Sunday. Jesus' death on the cross is the price tag that tells you how much you are worth—a price so high it can't be counted. That's how much God treasures you!

> You were bought, not with something that ruins
> like gold or silver, but with the precious blood
> of Christ, who was like a pure and perfect lamb.
>
> **1 PETER 1:18-19 NCV**

19. How can God have time for me when there are so many other people in the world?

People can think hard about just one thing at a time. God isn't like that. He knows everything all at once! He has a perfect understanding of everything that's going on with you—and everyone else—all at the same time.

Even though there are billions of people living on Earth right now, you are God's one-of-a-kind child. He saw you inside of your mom before you were born (Psalm 139:13-15). He knows your every thought (Psalm 139:2). He sees where you are every moment of every day (Psalm 139:3). He knows all about your future and has good plans for you (Psalm 139:16; also Jeremiah 29:11). Here's the best part: God not only *knows* about you—he *cares* about every detail of your life. Aren't you glad?

O Lord, you have examined my heart and know everything about me.

PSALM 139:1

20. Will God ever stop loving me?

Picture yourself enjoying a perfect day at the beach, running around in a special kind of sunshine that never bakes or burns you. Suddenly you get a nutty idea. You decide to run from that wonderful sun. You hurry inside, but you can't escape the sun's warmth. You lock yourself in a dark room, but light creeps in under the door. You discover that no matter where you go, the sunshine follows you.

Well, you may or may not try to run from the sun on the beach. But God's love is something you never want to run away from. And you can't! God's love is like that special sunshine. It reaches everywhere. It never stops reaching out to you.

> I am convinced that nothing can ever
> separate us from his love.
>
> **ROMANS 8:38**

21. Does God like my sister more than me?

Think you know someone who's perfect? Here's a secret: He's not! You might think that God is more pleased with a sister or brother or best friend than he is with you. Perhaps that person always seems to do and say the right thing.

But God doesn't have favorites. Here's why: Compared to each other, some of us might look better than others. But compared to God, no one looks good! Paul says that all of us have sinned and "fall short of God's glorious standard" (Romans 3:23). And Isaiah tells us that "all of us have strayed away like sheep" (Isaiah 53:6). We wander this way and that instead of following God and doing what he wants. The Lord knows that we all need his care and forgiveness. The truth is, we all mess up—but God still loves us all just the same.

> Remember that the heavenly Father to whom
> you pray has no favorites when he judges.
>
> **1 PETER 1:17**

QUESTIONS ABOUT PRAYER

Q:

22. Is God ever too busy to listen to my prayers?

A:

Sometimes the adults in your life are busy. You might hear a teacher or parent say, "Wait your turn." "Not now!" "After dinner." "Maybe this weekend." All of us know what it's like to have people tell us they are too busy to answer a question or to help us. Even grown-ups often hear from other grown-ups that they are too busy to talk or help.

But that's not how it is with God. Just as there is no end to how much God knows, there is no end to how much he cares and wants to help you. God is with you all the time. He doesn't take naps or watch TV or surf the Internet. He never feels tired from running the universe. He is so tuned in to you that he knows your every thought before you think it. He's listening even before you speak. So go ahead and pray. Tell God whatever you'd like to say. Whenever you want to talk, he's ready.

> Give all your worries and cares to God, for
> he cares about what happens to you.
>
> **1 PETER 5:7**

23. Is God really interested in my problems?

Picture yourself as a first-grader sitting at the kitchen table working on a word list. The words aren't much harder than *ball* and *dog*, but you're having a hard time. Then your older sister comes over and says, "I can help you with that." Your sister is a big help because she had to do this when she was in first grade too. And she knows more than you know. God is like that, only better! Because God sent his Son, Jesus, to Earth to live as a human being, you can trust that he understands everything that bothers you. He wants to help you with your problems, and he has the power to do it!

> People, trust God all the time. Tell him all your
> problems, because God is our protection.
>
> **PSALM 62:8 NCV**

24. Will God give me whatever I ask for when I pray?

Jesus said, "You can ask for anything in my name, and I will do it" (John 14:13). So Jesus did make an awesome promise to give us what we ask for. But that doesn't mean God is like a heavenly candy machine. You can't just put in a prayer, push the right button, and out pops your wish.

When God hears our prayers, he always answers. But he knows what is best for us, so he doesn't always answer exactly as we expect. We need to remember that Jesus said to "ask in his name." To ask in the name of Jesus means to tell God you want things that will bring him glory. What does that mean? It means that God will get the credit as we praise him for answering our prayers. So he answers in a way that shows how great he is. He answers by doing things that are good for us and all the other people in the world.

You can ask for anything in my name, and I will do it, because the work of the Son brings glory to the Father. Yes, ask anything in my name, and I will do it!

JOHN 14:13-14

QUESTIONS ABOUT JESUS

25. Did Jesus ever do anything wrong?

We must never picture Jesus as just another super-nice person, like a girl or boy at school who never talks out of turn or cuts into line. Jesus isn't just pretty good. He's the Son of God, and he's perfect!

When the enemies of Jesus wanted a reason to put him on the cross to die, they tried hard to find bad things he had done. They couldn't find any! So they asked people to lie and say bad things about Jesus (Matthew 26:59). But Peter said, "He never sinned" (1 Peter 2:22) and he is "the sinless, spotless Lamb of God" (1 Peter 1:19). Hebrews adds that he "did not sin" (4:15). Jesus always did what was right. He obeyed his Father perfectly, so he is a perfect example for us.

The chief priests and the whole Sanhedrin were looking for false evidence against Jesus so that they could put him to death. But they did not find any.

MATTHEW 26:59-60 NIV

26. Was Jesus ever tempted to sin?

Yep! The devil himself once tempted Jesus to show off his powers (Matthew 4:1-11). The Bible also says that Jesus "faced all of the same temptations we do" (Hebrews 4:15).

Temptation is a powerful pull to do something wrong. It's such a pesky part of everyday life that Jesus would not have been human if he had never felt tempted. Jesus was God, but he was also human like you and me. He faced the same strong tugs to do wrong that we do, but here's the difference: When you and I are tempted, we often give in. Jesus never did. That's great news. You can be sure Jesus understands what a struggle it is to keep from doing wrong. But you can also be sure he will help you keep from giving in to temptation!

> [Jesus] understands our weaknesses, for he faced all of the same temptations we do, yet he did not sin. So let us come boldly to the throne of our gracious God. There we will receive his mercy, and we will find grace to help us when we need it.
>
> **HEBREWS 4:15-16**

27. How can Jesus live inside me?

When you hear people say that Jesus "lives in your heart" it doesn't mean you have an itsy-bitsy man camping inside you. It means that when you trust in Jesus, he is present in your life. But he isn't just with you. He is so close that he is inside you. Now, it's a mystery exactly how Jesus can live inside each Christian, but we do know that he made this promise to his followers before he returned to heaven: "I am with you always" (Matthew 28:20).

Each time you let Jesus help you, you make him more and more welcome in your life. It's important to obey him when he helps you know in your heart what the right thing to do is. Jesus Christ living in you makes you a strong Christian!

I pray that Christ will be more and more at home in your hearts as you trust in him.

EPHESIANS 3:17

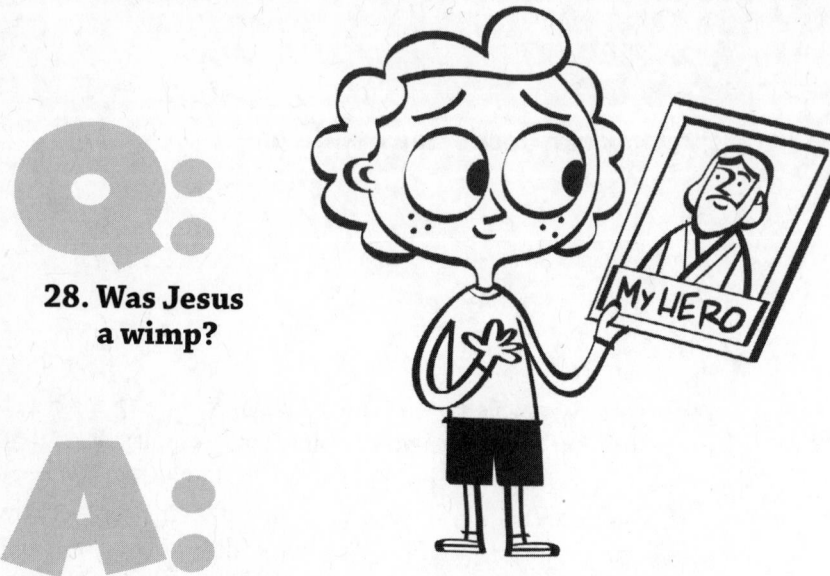

28. Was Jesus a wimp?

Some pictures of Jesus make him look pale and weak—like someone who maybe got beat up a lot growing up in his hometown of Nazareth. We don't know what Jesus looked like. It's true that he was a gentle poet and storyteller who bounced children on his knee. He helped sick people and those who were hungry and thirsty. But he also had the rough hands of a carpenter. He was able to live alone for a long time in the wilderness. He knocked over the tables of cheating businessmen. Then he was willing to go through a difficult death on the cross, but he also had the power to come back to life.

Can you picture him? Jesus is tender enough to care for your every need. But he is tough enough to be your all-powerful Savior.

> Jesus grew both in height and in wisdom, and
> he was loved by God and by all who knew him.
>
> **LUKE 2:52**

29. Did Jesus know he was God?

Many non-Christians agree that Jesus was one of the most important leaders who ever walked the Earth. They admit he was an excellent teacher of right and wrong—and an especially good person.

Jesus, however, claimed to be much more. He said he was God! Listen to this example, just one of many in the New Testament. Jesus said, "The Father and I are one" (John 10:30). The religious leaders understood exactly what he meant. They shouted, "You, a mere man, have made yourself God" (John 10:33). They picked up rocks to throw at him, trying to kill him. To everyone around Jesus, his claim to be God was shocking—shockingly clear!

> Jesus said, "At my Father's direction I have done many things to help the people. For which one of these good deeds are you killing me?" They replied, "Not for any good work, but for blasphemy, because you, a mere man, have made yourself God."
>
> **JOHN 10:32-33**

30. Did everyone in the Bible think Jesus was God?

Jesus is like a one-of-a-kind coin among billions and billions. Only Jesus perfectly fits every promise that God made about a Savior!

It's sad, but not everyone who met Jesus recognized him as God's Son, who came to be the Savior of the world. They should have! After all, God had said for hundreds of years that he would send a Savior to free his people from sin. The Old Testament has many special promises called prophecies. Long before Jesus was born, these prophecies described what the Savior would be like. He would be born in Bethlehem (Micah 5:2), do miracles (Isaiah 35:5-6), be betrayed by a friend (Psalm 41:9), have his hands and feet pierced (Psalm 22:16), suffer and die for our sins (Isaiah 53:5), and rise from the dead (Psalm 16:10).

Jesus perfectly fit not just a few, but hundreds of prophecies spoken hundreds of years before his birth. To anybody willing to see, this was powerful proof that Jesus was who he claimed to be!

> Even in his own land and among his own people, he was not accepted. But to all who believed him and accepted him, he gave the right to become children of God.
>
> **JOHN 1:12**

31. Did Jesus actually die on the cross—or did he just faint?

When Jesus rose from the dead, it was a one-of-a-kind event. It was so out of the ordinary that many people have said it couldn't possibly have happened. In fact, some say Jesus never even died on the cross. He just fainted, and in the cool air of the tomb he woke up and walked out.

But that's impossible to believe when you understand what Jesus went through the day he died. First the soldiers beat him. Then they nailed him to a cross. He hung there for six hours before he died. He was taken down from the cross only after a Roman soldier promised the Roman governor that he was dead. We can be sure that Jesus died. And we can be certain he came back to life.

God raised Jesus from the dead, and if God's Spirit is living in you, he will also give life to your bodies that die. God is the One who raised Christ from the dead, and he will give life through his Spirit that lives in you.

ROMANS 8:11 NCV

Q:

32. Did Jesus really come back to life after he died on the cross?

A:

Can you imagine a more astonishing miracle than a dead man coming back to life? The Bible tells us several big facts about the totally real rising again, or "resurrection," of Jesus.

First, Jesus died (John 19:28-37). Second, Jesus was buried (Luke 23:53). Third, Jesus really rose from the dead! You probably know that Jesus' closest friends found his empty tomb (Luke 24:1-7). Later his closest friends saw him alive (Luke 24:35-49). But did you know that Jesus also appeared to hundreds of people in his fully alive body (1 Corinthians 15:6)? Jesus wanted people to know his resurrection wasn't a crazy, made-up story. He wanted to make it easy, even for us today, to believe that he is alive.

I passed on to you what was most important and what had also been passed on to me—that Christ died for our sins, just as the Scriptures said. He was buried, and he was raised from the dead on the third day, as the Scriptures said.

1 CORINTHIANS 15:3-4

33. Could Jesus' disciples have made up the story about Jesus coming back to life?

If you wanted to know whether or not the moon is made of cheese, you would try to get information from people you could trust. You would need to hear the same facts from loads of people who had actually had a picnic on the moon, right? But what would make you really believe the truth would be finding people willing to die for their story—because people aren't willing to die for a lie.

That's the kind of wonderful proof we have that Jesus rose from the dead. Many people saw Jesus alive. They all reported the same facts. And each of them faced the danger of death for spreading the Good News about Jesus. The disciples didn't make up their story. They were star witnesses to the truth!

> This is that disciple who saw these events
> and recorded them here. And we all know that
> his account of these things is accurate.
>
> **JOHN 21:24**

I NEVER RIDE IN CARS BECAUSE I DON'T UNDERSTAND THEM!

34. How did Jesus come back to life?

No one understands exactly how God brought Jesus back to life. (After all, he's God and we're not!) But we can be sure it happened.

When Jesus came back to life, it was an event that was completely different from anything that had ever happened. A dead person had never before had the power to come to life and leave his grave. Lazarus had come out of his grave (John 11:38-44). But he hadn't done it alone—it was through Jesus' power.

After Jesus' body was placed in a tomb, we can be sure *what* happened—Jesus left the tomb, so it was empty. We know all about *who* did it—our Savior, Jesus. The Bible clearly explains *why* Jesus came back to life—this event provides proof of who he is. But *how* did Jesus do it? That's a mystery. In fact, it's a miracle! The Bible does say that God the Father raised up Jesus through the power of the Holy Spirit. The Spirit of God is the only power in the world big enough to win the battle over death.

> Jesus Christ our Lord was shown to be the Son of God when God powerfully raised him from the dead by means of the Holy Spirit.
>
> **ROMANS 1:4**

35. Is it okay to have Easter baskets and look for Easter eggs?

You dart behind a tree, pull apart the grass, and pop open a plastic egg. Out falls a bunch of jelly beans. Sounds fun! But people sometimes wonder if it's an okay thing to do on Easter. Any other day of the year it would be tough to knock a visit from a bunny that brings candy. Yet here's the problem: Sometimes the Easter Bunny turns into a bigger deal than Jesus—just like Santa Claus can crowd out the true message of Christmas. In whatever way your family celebrates Easter, your big job is to make Jesus the big deal. Easter is your special day to remember that Jesus rose from the dead. And that's even better than a basketful of jumbo-size chocolate bunnies!

The angel spoke to the women. "Don't be afraid!" he said. "I know you are looking for Jesus, who was crucified. He isn't here! He has been raised from the dead, just as he said would happen."

MATTHEW 28:5-6

QUESTIONS ABOUT THE HOLY SPIRIT

36. What's the Holy Spirit? Is he a ghost?

It might seem hard to understand what the Holy Spirit is like, but here's the big fact to remember: The Holy Spirit is God—along with God the Father and God the Son. Even though some Bibles call the Holy Spirit the "Holy Ghost," he isn't a ghost like you see in a cartoon or spooky movie. He's real and he's alive. He just doesn't have a body, so we can't see him. We say the Spirit of God is holy because he is perfect and pure, just like the Father and the Son.

> I will ask the Father, and he will give you another
> Helper to be with you forever—the Spirit of truth.
>
> **JOHN 14:16-17** NCV

Q:

37. How come I can't feel the Holy Spirit living in me?

A:

You can't see the wind, but you can see it sway the trees. You can't see the Holy Spirit, but you can tell that he is at work inside you. His presence in everyone who believes in Jesus is a fact (Ephesians 1:13).

And look at some of the great ways you can watch him help you grow: He makes you sure that God loves you (Romans 5:5). He helps you know Jesus better (Ephesians 3:19). He sets you free from sin (Romans 8:2). He teaches you right from wrong (John 16:8) and builds character in you (Galatians 5:22-23). He equips you with talents, abilities, and spiritual gifts so you can serve God (1 Corinthians 12:4,11). When you see those things beginning to happen in you, that's proof that the Holy Spirit is present in your life.

> When the Holy Spirit controls our lives, he will produce this kind of fruit in us: love, joy, peace, patience, kindness, goodness, faithfulness, gentleness, and self-control.
>
> **GALATIANS 5:22-23**

QUESTION ABOUT THE DEVIL

38. Is the devil real?

The devil (also called "Satan") is one of the first characters we meet in the Bible. He shows up as a serpent in the Garden of Eden to tempt Adam and Eve. He tells them it's okay to disobey God (Genesis 3:1-15). Some people picture the devil as nothing more than a fun-loving cartoon character with horns and long, red underwear, but he is very real. He wants to be powerful like God, and he wants us to join his fight against God. One of his big goals is to get people to sin. He tries to make *good* look bad and *bad* look good.

But the Bible has great news: "God's Spirit, who is in you, is greater than the devil, who is in the world" (1 John 4:4 NCV). That means the Holy Spirit can stop you from giving in to the devil's temptations. When you pray, the devil runs away!

> Resist the Devil and he will flee from you. Draw
> close to God, and God will draw close to you.
>
> **JAMES 4:7-8**

QUESTIONS ABOUT THE BIBLE

39. How do some people know so much about God?

Suppose you want to know all there is to know about the goliath bird-eating spider *(Theraphosa blondi)*, the world's largest spider. You would fly to the jungles of South America for a firsthand look at these hairy 11- to 12-inch monsters. You would study how they eat—and how they swallow. You might bring a baby spider home to your lab.

Well, if you want to know all about God, you need to try just as hard to see what you can learn. You read the Bible. You talk to God day by day about your struggles. You say thanks for God's gifts, obey him even when it's hard, and trust him to care for you always. You learn everything you can about God's Son, because he is just like his Father in heaven. There's no doubt about it: Soon you will know God very well. And his Son, Jesus, will not only be your Savior and your Master but your best Friend.

> I no longer call you servants, because
> a master doesn't confide in his
> servants. Now you are my friends.
>
> **JOHN 15:15**

40. Why is the Bible so big?

The Bible is a one-of-a-kind book—and it has a one-of-a-kind message. It tells us the things God wants us to know. It's a story stretching from the creation of the world until eternity, when we will live forever with God in heaven. It's filled with the history of how God and the humans he created have gotten along for thousands of years. It tells us how Jesus came to save us from sin and make us friends with God. And it's a map showing how to follow God's ways.

That's a lot to find inside one book! Since the Bible is such a huge book, one of the most important things you can do is to learn your way around. God will be pleased if you learn where some of your favorite Bible stories are written down.

Jesus' disciples saw him do many other miraculous signs besides the ones recorded in this book. But these are written so that you may believe that Jesus is the Messiah, the Son of God, and that by believing in him you will have life.

JOHN 20:30-31

41. How is the Bible different from other books?

The Bible is different from most books because it is really many smaller books in one—66, to be exact. More than 40 people helped write the Bible. The Bible was written over a long time—more than 1500 years. Its writers lived in Asia, Africa, and Europe and wrote in three different languages: Hebrew, Aramaic, and Greek.

Yet the Bible is different from all books in an even more important way: It is the totally true Word of God, the Creator of the whole universe. God had the writers put into the Bible exactly what he wanted us to know about himself. He gave us the Bible so we would know how we can trust God's Son, Jesus, and enjoy life that lasts forever with him in heaven. When we want to know how to live close to God, there's no other book like the Bible!

> You have been taught the holy Scriptures
> from childhood, and they have given you
> the wisdom to receive the salvation that
> comes by trusting in Christ Jesus.
>
> **2 TIMOTHY 3:15**

42. Why did God put his words in a book?

Suppose you carried a million dollars far into a forest and hid it deep in a mountain cave. If you wanted to be sure that you could find your cash years later, you wouldn't whisper the directions to your dog. You wouldn't trust them to your memory. You would write them down and make a map!

God wanted to share with us some very important directions—directions that are even more valuable than a treasure map for digging up a pile of money. God wanted us to be completely clear on how we can be his friend and obey him. So he wrote his instructions in a book to keep them safe. By putting into the Bible everything people need to know, God made sure we couldn't forget or mess up the message.

> The commandments of the LORD are right,
> bringing joy to the heart. The commands of
> the LORD are clear, giving insight to life.
>
> **PSALM 19:8**

LET'S START AT THE BEGINNING... CHAPTER ONE...

43. How could God write a book?

God didn't drop the Bible on us from heaven, wrapped in black leather and decorated with a big bow. Instead, God used people to write his book. But none of the writers just put down their own thoughts. They all wrote God's messages.

Sometimes God spoke out loud through prophets and told them to write down what he said. Other times the writers knew in their hearts what they should write. Either way, the message they passed on to us was God's. They spoke—and wrote—so we could know God's words.

> Above all, you must understand that no prophecy in Scripture ever came from the prophets themselves or because they wanted to prophesy. It was the Holy Spirit who moved the prophets to speak from God.
>
> **2 PETER 1:20-21**

44. Who wrote down the words in the Bible?

The words of God in the Bible were written down by kings, farmers, fishermen, poets, and even a doctor. The Bible is full of history and poetry and prayers and information. God made the most of each writer's personality and experience.

Solomon, for example, shared wisdom God had given him. David sang songs of praise. Prophets like Isaiah and Jeremiah comforted God's people—and warned them against sin. Hosea talked about his broken marriage to teach people about following God. You can think of each writer as an instrument God used to produce a beautiful song. Like the violins and trumpets and flutes and drums in an orchestra, each makes a different sound. Yet each plays a part in God's tune.

The LORD said to Moses,
"Write down these words."

EXODUS 34:27 NCV

45. How do we know the Bible is from God?

The Bible was written by some of God's best friends—Old Testament heroes like Moses, David, and Solomon, and New Testament followers of Jesus like John and Paul. It's surprising that all these people—who lived in different times and places—could write a book that makes any sense at all. Yet all of the Bible writers agree on hundreds of topics that people argue about.

Better yet, the Bible brings us one very special, very clear message about how God wants to save each of us through Jesus. That's a huge way in which we see that the Bible is more than a human book. It's God's Word. He put it together to tell us about himself. The Bible is "inspired by God" or "God-breathed" (NIV). It's packed by God with his powerful message that's worthy of our trust.

All Scripture is inspired by God.

2 TIMOTHY 3:16

46. The Bible is so old. How could it last so long?

When the writers of the Bible wrote down God's words, they didn't have computers or spiral notebooks. They wrote on materials like clay tablets, sheepskin, paper made from tall weeds, and calfskin.

The Bible writers handed their writings down to people who copied their work and kept it safe. As handwritten copies wore out, new ones were made and checked letter-by-letter to be sure there were no mistakes. God's people carefully guarded these Bibles in clay pots, caves, and churches so they would last a long time—hundreds and even thousands of years! So many handwritten copies were made that today we have thousands of these copies of different parts of the Bible. Some parts are almost as old as the first writings!

> People are like grass that dies away; their beauty
> fades as quickly as the beauty of wildflowers.
> The grass withers, and the flowers fall away.
> But the word of the Lord will last forever.
>
> **1 PETER 1:24-25**

47. Are parts of the Bible make-believe, or is everything true?

Even though Jesus lived 2000 years ago—and many Bible events happened long before he lived—everything in the Bible is real. The Bible writers knew the difference between make-believe and real life, and God gave each of them direction as they wrote carefully about their experiences with him.

Luke, for example, was a doctor who used reports from Jesus' closest followers and others who had been with him to write an organized summary of what Jesus said and did (Luke 1:1-4). And John tells us why he wrote carefully about the amazing miracles of Jesus and his awesome rising from the dead: so we could know for sure that when we believe in Jesus, he becomes our Savior (John 20:30-31).

The things that happened to those people are examples. They were written down to teach us.

1 CORINTHIANS 10:11 NCV

48. What will happen to people who don't obey the Bible?

Have you ever seen kids do bad stuff—big and little—and get away with it? Maybe you wish they would stop. Or maybe you wonder if you should join them.

Guess what? Anyone who disobeys God's commands in the Bible will come to a sad ending. God won't let people do wrong things forever. In Psalm 73:18 we read, "You put them on a slippery path and send them sliding over the cliff to destruction." We also read, "You are holding my right hand...How good it is to be near God! I have made the Sovereign LORD my shelter" (verses 23,28). So while you wait for evil to come to an end, keep doing what's right and trusting God to take care of you. It's smart to be on God's side!

> I was jealous of proud people. I saw wicked people doing well...Then I understood what will happen to them. You have put them in danger; you cause them to be destroyed.
>
> **PSALM 73:3,17-18 NCV**

49. Why is the Bible so hard to understand?

Suppose you decide to read the Bible from cover to cover. You flip to Genesis 1:1. You read all about creation. That's not tough. Soon you reach stories you've heard in Sunday school—about Noah and Abraham and Joseph and Moses. They're easy too. Then suddenly you're reading about animal offerings, and directions for making a worship place called a tabernacle, and page after page of strange rules. If you keep going, you stumble over tribes and kings and visions.

Yes, the Bible is a big book with lots for us to learn—enough to study for a lifetime, in fact. But the Bible is full of truths you *can* understand. It's packed with commands you can obey today. And it's filled with wisdom you need right now. How do you find the best parts to read? Look up the verses from this book. And ask an adult who knows the Bible well for some other great parts to read!

Your word is a lamp
for my feet and a
light for my path.

PSALM 119:105

50. Why does the Bible have so many rules?

The Bible might seem like it's just full of rules. But the Bible is filled with many other things too. It's packed with words of praise, wise sayings to live by, and loads of history. It tells the story of how God wants to be our friend—and how he sent Jesus to save us. And yes, large sections of the Bible have rules from God, telling us how he wants us to live.

But all of the Bible's rules fit under two main rules. Jesus said that the two most important commandments are these: First, "You must love the Lord your God with all your heart, all your soul, and all your mind." And second, "Love your neighbor as yourself." If you remember those two rules and obey them, you'll be obeying all the rules of the Bible!

> Jesus replied, "'You must love the Lord your God with all your heart, all your soul, and all your mind.' This is the first and greatest commandment. A second is equally important: 'Love your neighbor as yourself.'"
>
> **MATTHEW 22:37-39**

51. Are the Bible's rules old-fashioned?

Some people think that the Bible's commands must be out-of-date. After all, the Bible was written before cars, computers, and cable TV. Yet reading the Bible is like looking in a mirror. From cover to cover you read stuff that talks about you and your world in its pages.

And it's clear that we still need God's rules. Take the Ten Commandments (Exodus 20:1-17). People still have problems with stealing, lying, whining to their parents, and wishing they had their neighbors' toys. Kids on the playground still swear, using God's name disrespectfully. And all of us still forget from time to time to make God more important than anyone or anything else in our lives. God didn't make rules that would only work for a while in the old days—and not be important today. He makes rules that last.

> Long ago I learned from your rules that
> you made them to continue forever.
>
> **PSALM 119:152** NCV

52. Is the Bible always right?

Parents may make mistakes when they help you with your homework. Teachers might have to say, "I don't know" when you ask a question and power up an encyclopedia on the Web to find answers.

But there's one source of information that is always available and always has the correct answers: the Bible. In Proverbs 30:5 we read that "every word of God proves true." Second Timothy 3:16 tells us that "all Scripture is inspired by God and is useful to teach us what is true and to make us realize what is wrong in our lives. It straightens us out and teaches us to do what is right." The Bible isn't just a good book full of interesting stories. It's a special book full of God's perfect directions. You can count on the Bible to help you learn how to become friends with God and live the right way!

> All he does is just and good, and all his
> commandments are trustworthy. They are
> forever true, to be obeyed faithfully.
>
> **PSALM 111:7-8**

53. Why are there so many different kinds of Bibles?

Take a look around your church or a Christian bookstore and you'll see Bibles in all sizes and colors. Flip those Bibles open and you'll find that many have notes to help you study God's Word. Start to read and you'll discover the biggest difference of all: Various Bibles use different words to say the same verse. Even so, the message stays the same. It was written thousands of years ago, mostly in the Hebrew and Greek languages.

Today the whole Bible has been written in almost 400 different languages so that people all over the world can understand it. In English there are dozens of versions that start with the original Hebrew and Greek words of the Bible (but probably just a few versions are used at your church). Each of them tries to say the original words in ways that are clear. That's why different versions of the Bible can sound so different!

Heaven and earth
will disappear, but
my words will
remain forever.

MATTHEW 24:35

QUESTIONS ABOUT DIFFERENT RELIGIONS

54. Why do people from different religions sometimes fight?

One peek at the news on TV or the Internet tells you that people from different religions don't always get along. Followers of various religions sometimes argue and fight, trying to make others accept their faith. Some even hurt and kill others because they hate people who don't believe the way they do.

The Bible shows us a different way of getting people to believe the truth of who Jesus is. We are to tell others about Jesus by explaining how great he is and telling what he has done for us. Here's how Peter explains it: "You were chosen to tell about the wonderful acts of God, who called you out of darkness into his wonderful light" (1 Peter 2:9 NCV). Telling others about Jesus is about giving people reasons to believe—and loving them, not getting angry with them.

> Worship Christ as Lord of your life. And
> if you are asked about your Christian hope,
> always be ready to explain it. But you must
> do this in a gentle and respectful way.
>
> **1 PETER 3:15-16**

55. Does my Muslim friend pray to the same God I do?

The kids at your school or in your neighborhood probably don't all go to church. At least a few of them might be Muslim, Hindu, Buddhist, or followers of some other religion. Some people say you and your friends all pray to the same God—like you're sending smoke up different chimneys into the same big sky.

That sounds cool. But it's not true. Jesus said that his Father is "the only true God" (John 17:3) and that no one gets to God except through him (John 14:6). As a Christian, you know the living, loving God of the Bible. You have an exciting opportunity to share the truth about God with your non-Christian friends!

> There is one God and one way human beings can reach God. That way is through Christ Jesus...He gave himself as a payment to free all people.
>
> **1 TIMOTHY 2:5-6 NCV**

56. Do I have to tell people about Jesus?

Did you know that you have been given the most important job on Earth? Yes, you! If you have trusted in Jesus as your Savior, then God has appointed you to be his messenger. He asks you to spread the Good News that he wants to be friends with everyone in the world—and that he offers forgiveness in Jesus. It's one of the biggest commands Jesus ever gave. He said to "go into all the world and preach the Good News to everyone, everywhere" (Mark 16:15).

God doesn't expect you to do the job alone. He has surrounded you with other Christians who have the same job, and Jesus himself promises to always be with you. Telling others about Jesus is a task God commands you to do. But it's also a job you should be glad that God allows you to do for him.

Go and make disciples of all the nations, baptizing them in the name of the Father and the Son and the Holy Spirit. Teach these new disciples to obey all the commands I have given you. And be sure of this: I am with you always, even to the end of the age.

MATTHEW 28:19-20

Q:

57. Does it matter which God people believe in?

A:

At the time the Bible was written, people worshiped many different gods. Yet those who wrote the Bible said that there is only one God worth believing in. In Exodus 34:14 we read, "You must worship no other gods, but only the LORD, for he is a God who is passionate about his relationship with you." And Acts 4:12 makes it very clear why believing in the God of the Bible matters so much: "Jesus is the only One who can save people. His name is the only power in the world that has been given to save people. We must be saved through him" (NCV).

If we really want to know God, we need to know the one real God—and his real plan to make us his friends!

> How great you are, O Sovereign LORD! There
> is no one like you—there is no other God.
>
> **2 SAMUEL 7:22**

QUESTIONS ABOUT RIGHT AND WRONG

58. Can I decide for myself what's right and wrong?

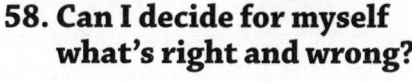

Think about what it would be like to be in the middle of a board game when everyone started to make up new rules. The game would fall apart. Suddenly the fun would be over.

It's exactly like that when people try to decide right and wrong for themselves. Even though it sounds great to make your own rules, people get along far better when we have rules we can count on—rules that don't change, rules made by someone who knows what is best for everyone. Because God is wise and totally unselfish, he makes perfect rules. He makes these rules clear in the Bible. He loves you too much to leave it up to you to pick right and wrong!

> The word of the Lord holds true, and everything
> he does is worthy of our trust.
> He loves whatever is just and good, and
> his unfailing love fills the earth.
>
> **PSALM 33:4-5**

59. Why do we need rules?

Roller-coaster lovers are smart enough to climb inside the roller-coaster cars—not step in front of them. Softball fans know that bats are for pounding balls—not people. Hockey players aim for the other team's goal—not their own. Get it? Even when we do the things we love to do, there are all sorts of rules to help us make the most of our fun.

God's commands work the same way. God never makes rules to give us trouble. Jesus, in fact, told us his real goal: "My purpose," he said, "is to give life in all its fullness" (John 10:10). God loves you so much that he gives you his clear commands to show you the very best way to enjoy life.

> Your word is a lamp for my feet and a light for my path. I've promised it once, and I'll promise again: I will obey your wonderful laws.
>
> **PSALM 119:105-106**

60. Does God punish me when I do wrong?

No—and yes. When Jesus died on the cross for you, he canceled forever the punishment you deserve (Isaiah 53:4-9). Because God has forgiven you, there's no longer a need for you to take the blame for your sins.

But that doesn't mean you escape the results that come from bad actions. If you don't do your homework, you earn a low grade. If you refuse to wear a bike helmet, sooner or later you bonk your head. If you bug your sister, she's likely to bug you back. So you still get hurt in some ways for doing wrong. And you still need to ask God to forgive you. Yet God's purpose isn't to pound on you. He isn't out to get you for being bad but to teach you that it's always best to choose to do good.

My child, don't ignore it when the Lord disciplines
you, and don't be discouraged when he corrects you.
For the Lord disciplines those he loves, and he
punishes those he accepts as his children.

HEBREWS 12:5-6

61. Why is it sometimes easier to do things that are wrong than to do what's right?

Sit on a chair and try a simple experiment: Slide your bottom off the seat of the chair. What happens? You always fall on the floor. Why? Because you can't undo the power of gravity—the force that pulls you down.

It's the same way when it comes to trying in your own strength to overcome the pull of sin. Inside you and every other human being there is a power at work—your sinful nature—that makes it far easier for you to do wrong than right (Galatians 5:17). Yet as a Christian there's an even bigger force at work in you to help you do right: the Holy Spirit. It's the job of the Holy Spirit to help you understand God's commands and obey them. With the Spirit's help, you don't have to do things that are wrong. You can choose to do right!

> I advise you to live according to your new
> life in the Holy Spirit. Then you won't be
> doing what your sinful nature craves.
>
> **GALATIANS 5:16**

62. How does God help me choose to do the right thing?

God doesn't ask you to do the job of making right choices all alone. He gives you his Word to teach you right from wrong (Psalm 119:105). He shows you how to escape temptation (1 Corinthians 10:13).

He also helps in a way you might not have thought of: by promising to meet your every need (Philippians 4:19). That is God's big way of getting rid of your reasons to do wrong. God knows you need friends, for example, and he will show you how to get friends without doing bad stuff to wow them. He knows you need to do well in school, and he will help you study and do your best without cheating. As you live close to God—telling him about your problems and asking him to meet your needs—he will help you. You never have to do bad things to get God's good stuff!

> His divine power has given us everything
> we need for life and godliness.
>
> **2 PETER 1:5 NIV**

63. Why do I sometimes get in trouble for doing the right thing?

"No one rules unless God has given him the power to rule," says Paul in Romans 13:1 (NCV). God puts people in charge of you—like parents, teachers, and police—because he plans for them to protect and provide for you. He gives them power to reward good deeds and punish bad ones (Romans 13:3-4).

Sometimes, however, people in charge make mistakes and punish good people. Some use their power in wrong ways and hurt people who do right. A few even pick on Christians (Luke 21:17; John 15:20-21). Whether you get in trouble for something you didn't do or just for believing in Jesus, you can obey God by always doing the right thing. You can start by showing respect for the people in charge of you and praying for them!

> If people persecute you because you are a
> Christian, don't curse them; pray that God will
> bless them...Never pay back evil for evil to anyone.
>
> **ROMANS 12:14,17**

64. Why do some Christians not act like Christians?

There's a big word in the Bible for a person who says he is a Christian but doesn't act like one: *hypocrite* (HIP-uh-krit). It comes from the name for ancient Greek actors, who were famous for the masks they hid behind. It's what Jesus called the religious people who acted good on the outside but were full of sin on the inside (Matthew 23:25-27). He got very angry with them—not for sinning once, twice, or even many times but for pretending to be good when they weren't. Hypocrites act the way they do because they aren't close friends with God.

Sometimes hypocrites say they are Christians but do unkind things to other people. When non-Christians see that, they think all Christians are fakes. Being a hypocrite is the exact opposite of what Jesus wants us to be. So don't ever be a pretender. Be a believer who loves Jesus through and through, and show it by the way you act!

> Be sure that you live in a way that brings
> honor to the Good News of Christ.
>
> **PHILIPPIANS 1:27** NCV

QUESTIONS ABOUT THE FUTURE

65. Does God know what my life will be like when I grow up?

David once told God, "You saw me before I was born. Every day of my life was recorded in your book. Every moment was laid out before a single day had passed" (Psalm 139:16). Wow! God knows every deed you will do, every word you will speak, and every breath you will take.

God not only knows all about your whole life, but he has an awesome plan for your future. The most important part of his plan is for you to become an excited follower of Jesus, and that's something you can start on right now. Each time you learn about God's clear commands in the Bible—and each time you obey them—you are one step further along in becoming the person God plans for you to be!

We can make our plans, but the
LORD determines our steps.

PROVERBS 16:9

66. Does God care what job I have when I grow up?

God cares about everything that's important to you—especially something as huge as the 300 million seconds you will spend working as a grown-up. Perhaps you will get a job in an office or a store, work in a hospital or at a church, or start your own business. You may become a farmer or carpenter, travel as a salesperson, work at home caring for a family, or become a missionary. Whatever work you choose to do as an adult, this is one of the biggest decisions you will ever make.

And God has a plan for you. In Ephesians 2:10 we read, "We are God's masterpiece. He has created us anew in Christ Jesus, so that we can do the good things he planned for us long ago." God made you his special work of art—a one-of-a-kind bundle of gifts—and he decided long ago what good work you would do!

> Whatever you do, work at it with all your
> heart, as working for the Lord.
>
> **COLOSSIANS 3:23 NIV**

67. Will God tell me what will happen in my future?

There's no doubt that God knows about your future. He has an awesome plan for your life. The big question is how much he plans to tell you—and when.

Actually, God wants to tell you a whole lot about your future, but he is too wise to tell you all of it at once. He will tell you only what you need to know exactly when you can handle it! For example, you don't need to know in third grade—or even in sixth grade—where you'll go to college, what you'll do for a job, if you'll get married, or when and where you'll retire! God lovingly chooses to keep your future a secret. But as you ask him to help you make right choices—starting now—he will show you his plan for your life one step at a time!

> Trust in the Lord with all your heart; do not depend on your own understanding. Seek his will in all you do, and he will direct your paths.
>
> **PROVERBS 3:5-6**

68. Why does God let bad things happen to me sometimes?

Sometimes bad things happen to you because of your own poor choices—like gulping pool water because you jumped in over your head without knowing how to swim. Some hurtful things come because of other people's bad choices—like getting hit by a driver talking on a cell phone. And other bad stuff—like sickness, storms, and earthquakes—just happens because we live in a world that's not perfect.

When you're hurt or sad, remember this: Jesus made a wonderful promise to be with you through anything and everything (Matthew 28:20). And he will use the bad things that happen to help you trust him more. He wants you to know that you can count on him no matter what you go through!

> There is wonderful joy ahead, even though it
> is necessary for you to endure many trials
> for a while. These trials are only to test your
> faith, to show that it is strong and pure.
>
> **1 PETER 1:6-7**

69. Can God make bad things turn out okay?

When bad things happen to you, God promises to do a surprising thing: make good come out of bad! When you love God, he makes everything in your life happen the way he plans it (Romans 8:28). That doesn't mean that God will always help you get right out of bed when

you're sick. And he won't help you remember math facts you didn't take the time to learn. Sometimes God does quickly save you from your troubles, but not always.

But there is one good thing God plans to bring out of every bad thing you face: He wants to help you learn to think and act like his Son, Jesus (Romans 8:29). God always helps you and holds you in his arms when you hurt. And the very best thing he is doing for you is making sure that everything that happens in your life helps you become more like Jesus!

> We know that God causes everything to work together for the good of those who love God and are called according to his purpose for them. For God knew his people in advance, and he chose them to become like his Son.
>
> **ROMANS 8:28-29**

QUESTIONS ABOUT CHURCH

70. Why do we go to church?

When you trusted Jesus to be your Savior, God made you part of the church. No, he didn't turn you into a brick. He made you a member of what the Bible calls the "body of Christ" (1 Corinthians 12:12-13, 26-27). He joined you to a huge group—all of Jesus' followers from around the world.

You probably get together often with part of that group—the church family that attends worship services in your local church building. We need each other! The Holy Spirit gives each of us a job to do to help each other grow closer to Jesus. He gives us jobs like serving, encouraging, giving, teaching, and leading (Romans 12:6-8; 1 Corinthians 12:4-11). And just like your body doesn't work well without all its parts, the body of Christ (the church) doesn't work well unless each of us joins in!

What happens to a coal that rolls away from a campfire and stays by itself?

We are all parts of his one body, and each of us has different work to do. And since we are all one body in Christ, we belong to each other, and each of us needs all the others.

ROMANS 12:5

71. Why does church last so long?

That's a funny question. Have you ever heard anyone wonder why parties last so long? Probably not. God didn't plan for us to be miserable at church. He wants every get-together among Christians to be a time to celebrate! Church is a total bore only when leaders up front or people in the pews forget why they're there.

A worship service at church is a special time to enjoy our friendship with each other and, most of all, with God. If you ever start to snooze at church, wake yourself up with this fact: The Bible commands you to hang out with God's people so you can keep encouraging each other to become better and better friends with him!

> We should not stop gathering together with other
> believers, as some of you are doing. Instead, we
> must continue to encourage each other even more.
>
> **HEBREWS 10:25 GWT**

72. My friend doesn't go to church—what should I do?

A friend who doesn't go to church could be a Christian who is missing out on the awesome, growing friendship she could have with Jesus—and some of his followers. Or maybe a friend who picks soccer or sleeping in over Sunday school has never trusted Jesus.

Either way, church might not sound like much fun to your friend. But as this kid watches you live your life close to Jesus, sooner or later she will wonder how you got so tight with God. And that's your chance to invite your friend to come along to worship, Sunday school, or another activity—not just to meet your great friends or be part of a group, but to get to really know and believe in Jesus!

> You were chosen to tell about the wonderful acts of God, who called you out of darkness into his wonderful light. At one time you were not a people, but now you are God's people.
>
> **1 PETER 2:9-10 NCV**

QUESTIONS ABOUT DEATH AND HEAVEN

73. Why did my grandma die when the Bible says that Christians will live forever?

No one escapes death, not even Christians. Younger people some-times die because of accidents or sickness. Older people can die from accidents or disease too, but many die simply because their bodies wear out. We feel sad when people die, because we miss them.

But here's the important fact: Death isn't the end for us. Even when we die, the most important part of us keeps liv-ing. It's the part we can't see—our "spirit" or "soul." That part of Christians will live forever. Jesus said, "I am the resurrec-tion and the life. Those who believe in me, even though they die like everyone else, will live again" (John 11:25). What a promise! Everyone who trusts in Jesus will live forever!

I [Jesus] tell you the truth, whoever hears what
I say and believes in the One who sent me has
eternal life. That person will not be judged guilty
but has already left death and entered life.

JOHN 5:24 NCV

74. What will I look like in heaven?

Guess what? You'll still be you—only better! The Bible says your spirit will live forever. But it also promises you'll get a new body to live in.

Right now we all have "earthly bodies" that die (1 Corinthians 15:42). But in heaven we will get "spiritual bodies" that last forever (1 Corinthians 15:42,44). God will take the bodies we have now and "change them into glorious bodies like his own, using the same mighty power that he will use to conquer everything, everywhere" (Philippians 3:21). Your new body will be filled with the same power that raised Jesus from the dead. It will be like the body Jesus got after he came back to life—not because it comes with a beard and long hair but because it won't ever break or wear out—or die!

> Our earthly bodies, which die and decay, will be different when they are resurrected, for they will never die...They are natural human bodies now, but when they are raised, they will be spiritual bodies. For just as there are natural bodies, so also there are spiritual bodies.
>
> **1 CORINTHIANS 15:42,44**

75. Will everybody go to heaven?

There's only one way people can go to heaven when they die. It's by trusting Jesus while they are alive. Everyone who trusts Jesus will live forever in heaven with God. People who say no to God's gift of forgiveness will live away from God and his people forever (John 5:24-29; Matthew 25:31-46).

God's biggest desire is for people to turn away from their sins—the bad things they do—and come back to him. They can do this by trusting Jesus as their Savior, admitting he is the only one who can forgive them and help them become friends with God. We should be eager to tell others about Jesus, so we can bring as many people with us to heaven as we can!

> The Lord isn't really being slow about his promise to return, as some people think. No, he is being patient for your sake. He does not want anyone to perish, so he is giving more time for everyone to repent.
>
> **2 PETER 3:9**

FOREVER WITH JESUS!

76. How long will we be in heaven?

That's an easy one. Forever! One of the most famous verses in the Bible says this: "God so loved the world that he gave his only Son, so that everyone who believes in him will not perish but have eternal life" (John 3:16). The word *eternal* means something that will never end. Jesus promised that he was going to prepare a place for us. He said, "I will come and get you, so that you will always be with me where I am" (John 14:3).

Here's the hard part. We can't begin to get our brains to understand the fact that we will live in heaven always and forever. But we can get this much: Eternal life isn't just about having lungs that work for a really long time. It's about having a heart that will love forever the Lord of the universe—your best-ever friend, Jesus!

> And so we will be with the Lord forever.
>
> **1 THESSALONIANS 4:17 NiV**

77. How do I know I'm going to heaven?

Good question! In fact, Jesus' best friends asked him the same thing. Jesus said there is just one way to get to his Father's home in heaven—and he is it! Jesus declared that *he* is the way.

It may seem strange to think of a person as a path, but Jesus is saying, "If you want to get to heaven, the only way to get there is by believing in me." Jesus made a very special promise to his followers. He said, "I assure you, those who listen to my message and believe in God who sent me have eternal life" (John 5:24). He was saying that if we believe in God and follow Jesus, we'll live forever! Those are directions you can count on to get you to God's home!

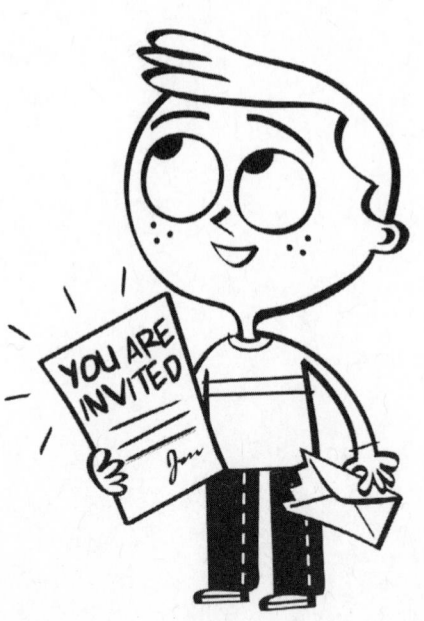

Jesus told him, "I am the way, the truth, and the life. No one can come to the Father except through me."

JOHN 14:6

Learning and Conversation
Guide for Parents

QUESTIONS ABOUT GOD

1. Why did God make people?

Learn it. Show your child the story of Adam and Eve at the very beginning of the Bible (Genesis 1:27-31). Point out ways we see that God was friends with Adam and Eve: God talked with them, provided food for them, and gave both of them someone they could enjoy being with—each other! Even more exciting is what the *end* of the Bible says about God's plan for us to be friends with him forever. You may want to read this special description of heaven with your child: "Look, the home of God is now among his people! He will live with them, and they will be his people. *God himself will be with them*" (Revelation 21:3).

2. How do we know what God is like when we can't see him?

Draw it. Read Luke 18:15-17 to your child. Provide clay or crayons and paper so your child can create a picture of that story. Talk about how kind Jesus was to the children. And name some things we discover about God by learning what Jesus was like.

QUESTIONS ABOUT SIN

3. Why do I feel bad when I do something wrong?

Act it. Ask your child to playact this situation: "Pretend you did something wrong. Show what it looks like when you *don't* feel sorry."

(Ideas: Make a face, stick out a tongue, and skip around as if everything is okay.) "Now show what being sorry looks like." (Ideas: Hang head down, look sad, and quiver lips.) Talk about this truth: "God doesn't want us just to *look* sorry when we do something wrong. He wants us to feel bad so that we'll admit our sin to him. Then he wants us to do whatever we can to fix what we did wrong, and we'll be happy again!"

4. What if I don't feel bad when I do something wrong?

Share it. Share with your family how God's Word has helped you learn right from wrong. How has it been a better guide than your feelings have been?

5. Why does sin keep me from being friends with God?

Compare it. Say, "Imagine you were playing outside and your shoes were covered with mud. What might I say if you wanted to walk into the house wearing your muddy shoes?" Explain that you might say something like this: "I can't let you come into the house with dirty shoes. But I don't want you to have to stay outside forever. I want you in the house with me. So you have to take off those dirty shoes!" Point out that this is how it is with God. "Our sins keep us away from God, but he forgives us. That gets rid of our sins, just like taking off dirty shoes gets rid of the mud. When our sins are gone, we can be near God. We can talk to him whenever we want to because he is right with us."

6. Why does God say the punishment for sin is death?

Compare it. As you walk through a mall or drive by a car dealership, point out some high-ticket items (a row of jumbo TVs, for example, or a car lot filled with new cars). Take the opportunity to say, "Those are really expensive items. They cost a huge amount of money. But Jesus paid an even bigger price to save us from being punished for our sin. He paid for our sin with his own life!"

7. Why doesn't God just forget our sins?

Ask it. To help communicate our need for forgiveness, ask your child, "How would you feel if a classmate always pulled your hair and pushed you down but was never punished?" Then ask, "Do you think the wrong things that you do should be punished?" And finish with, "How does it make you feel that Jesus took the punishment for your sin so that you could be forgiven?" Talk about why forgiving is even better than forgetting. Discuss the fact that a forgiven sin is gone, not just forgotten.

8. Are "little" sins okay with God?

Compare it. Use humor to point out the warped logic of this question by rewording it. Come up with comparisons like these: Is it okay to bang my right thumb with a hammer so long as I don't hit my left thumb? Is it okay to drink drain cleaner if I only drink half the bottle? Can I smoke if I only smoke a pack a day? Talk about how silly it is to ask if it's okay to do something just a little stupid. Point out that if something is bad, it's bad even if you don't do it too much. And if we really love God, we show it by not trying to get away with sins—even "little" ones.

9. Why is sin sometimes fun?

Ask it. Talk about these questions with your child: "When does sin feel 'fast, easy, and free'?" "What happens to sinful people in the long run?" Then talk about the opposite: "What good things happen when we choose to do the right thing—even if it's 'slow, hard, and costly'?"

QUESTIONS ABOUT FORGIVENESS

10. Why did Jesus die?

Learn it. This is the most important part of the Good News. Jesus was our stand-in. He died in our place, taking the punishment we had coming. Here's another key verse to share with your child: "He was handed over to die because of our sins, and he was raised from the dead to make us right with God" (Romans 4:25).

11. Why did Jesus have to die for my sin when I haven't done anything really bad?

Live it. When children think their sins are "no big deal," it often means they believe that the wrong things they do seem small compared to the terrible things others do. When your child does something wrong, help him or her pray a simple two-step prayer: 1) admitting sin to God, and 2) thanking God for his forgiveness. Without owning up to sin, a child doesn't grapple with the wrong he has done. Without getting hold of God's forgiveness, he remains burdened by guilt. Your child can remember this two-step process by memorizing today's verse.

12. Will God forgive really bad people?

Act it. Whether we look "good" or "bad" to the people around us, all of our sins require the same solution. Ask your child, "If you were God, what would you say to us sinners?" Prompt your child to play-act saying things they would say but God wouldn't, such as, "You're so terrible that I won't let you near me." "Your sins are too big to forgive." "Jesus didn't die for you." Then act out some simple scenes in which your child says some things God *would* say. For example: "I love you so much I planned a way for you to be near me." "My Son, Jesus, died for every one of your sins." "My love for you is bigger than anything bad you have done."

13. Does God always forgive me?

Compare it. Here is an analogy you can use to help your child better understand God's forgiveness: "Our friendship with God is like a beautiful vase. Sin is like knocking that vase to the ground—or throwing it at a wall. As humans, the best we can do is glue the vase back together and hope the cracks don't show. God does a far better thing. His forgiveness glues all the broken pieces of our friendship back together. We get a fresh start with him. A good-as-new friendship. It's as if we never sinned. All the cracks are gone!"

QUESTIONS ABOUT GOD'S LOVE

14. How do I know God wants to be my friend?

Draw it. Have your child draw a flock of sheep and print John 10:14-15 on the paper. Talk about ways a shepherd helps sheep and ways that Jesus, our Shepherd, helps us.

15. What kind of friend is God?

Compare it. Have your child take a sheet of paper and write this verse at the top: "God is love" (1 John 4:8). List ways God shows his love to you. Then list people who remind you of God. Here are some examples: "God always loves me like Grandma"; "God gives food to me like Mom and Dad"; "God is always patient like my friend _____"; and so on. At the bottom of the paper, write these words: "God is the best friend of all!"

16. Does God love me more when I obey him?

Ask it. The next time your child feels wronged by a friend or family member, talk about how sad and upset he or she feels. Ask, "How do you wish _____ had treated you? Why would that be better than how _____ did treat you?" Explain, "That's how God feels when we sin. He forgives us, but he still feels sad. He is upset when we hurt each other. He knows that obeying him is the best thing we can do."

17. How can I be better friends with God?

Live it. Is your child building a habit of spending time with God each day? If not, here's a simple way to get going: On small slips of paper write the references for Bible verses you want your child to learn—starting with short, one- or two-verse passages. Put these slips of paper in a cup, and draw a slip each day after dinner or before bedtime. Look up the verse, read it, and ask what that verse had to do with life that day. Ask about your child's "highs" and "lows" of the day, and pray about the things you discuss.

18. How much does God love me?

Compare it. Talk with your child about your family's most treasured possession—pictures, hobby equipment, your home, and so on. Why does this thing mean so much to you? How would you feel if you lost it? Then explain, "We really value _____. But God's love for us is far more valuable. He loves us a zillion times more than we could ever love."

19. How can God have time for me when there are so many other people in the world?

Draw it. Read Psalm 139:1-18 together. As you read, make a list of everything God knows about you. Then encourage your child to draw pictures of some of the things you listed. This will be a great reminder of God's incredible care for each of us.

20. Will God ever stop loving me?

Learn it. Read all of Romans 8:38-39—and make it your project to memorize this great passage as a family: "I am convinced that nothing can ever separate us from his love. Death can't, and life can't. The angels can't, and the demons can't. Our fears for today, our worries about tomorrow, and even the powers of hell can't keep God's love away. Whether we are high above the sky or in the deepest ocean, nothing in all creation will ever be able to separate us from the love of God that is revealed in Christ Jesus our Lord."

21. Does God like my sister more than me?

Act it. Line up your family to compare who is tallest—and shortest. Point out that the differences in height seem like a big deal. Then ask, "What if we were standing next to a 100-story building? Would any of us look very big?" Explain that you would all realize you are very small and your differences are tiny. It's the same way with trying to see who pleases God the most. Next to him, none of us measures up, but he loves every one of us anyway!

QUESTIONS ABOUT PRAYER

22. Is God ever too busy to listen to my prayers?

Live it. Make it a family practice to recognize that God is available to us 24/7. You can do this by practicing "popcorn prayers." As needs and concerns and points for praise arise, take time for brief prayers with your child. Explain, "You know, we don't have to wait until dinnertime (or family devotions or bedtime) to talk to God about that. Let's pray about it right now."

23. Is God really interested in my problems?

Live it. You can show each other God's always-available love by making a fresh effort to pay attention to each other's concerns. Here's one way to start: Talk about the fact that many of us do bad things to get attention when we feel others are not paying attention to us. Decide together on a positive phrase that family members can use when they need some help. When someone hears this phrase from a family member, the two of them should stop and talk to God together, asking him for wisdom on how to handle the problem. Try these: "I've got a 9-1-1 for God." Or just, "Can we talk to God about this?"

24. Will God give me whatever I ask for when I pray?

Ask it. Your child needs to know that God is eager to hear about our hurts, needs, and desires. But talk with your child about this question: "How can we pray so we aren't treating God Like a candy machine? What can we ask for that would be good for us and all the other people in our lives—and bring God glory?"

QUESTIONS ABOUT JESUS

25. Did Jesus ever do anything wrong?

Ask it. Ask your child, "How does it make you feel knowing that Jesus never did anything wrong? How does it help you to know that Jesus was perfect?" Talk about the fact that Jesus became our Savior when he died on the cross. But during the time when he was alive on Earth, he also was a wonderful example for us. The Bible tells us to "fix our eyes on Jesus" (Hebrews 12:2 NIV). That means we should look at what Jesus did and learn to be like him.

26. Was Jesus ever tempted to sin?

Act it. Ask your child if she can name some temptations she faces in everyday life. Then read 1 Corinthians 10:13, which promises that in the midst of a temptation God always provides a way out. Role-play some temptations your child faces, pointing out how she can always ask Jesus for help by praying anywhere at any time. Name some ways

Jesus might help your child escape powerful pulls to do wrong, such as providing a friend who also doesn't want to give in to temptation.

27. How can Jesus live inside me?

Share it. Talk with your child about how you have sensed Jesus living in you, helping you understand and obey God. Perhaps you want to tell how he helped you make the right decision about what to study, what job to take, who to marry, where to live, where to go to church, how to be obedient to God in a difficult situation, and so on.

28. Was Jesus a wimp?

Ask it. Read the passage above to your child, then ask, "What do you think it was like to grow up around Jesus?" Follow up with this: "What qualities do you think made Jesus lovable to both God and people? What does the Bible tell us about the kind of person Jesus was?"

29. Did Jesus know he was God?

Learn it. Explain that in John 10 *blasphemy* means claiming to be God when you're just a human person. But Jesus *is* God, and he knew it. Read Philippians 2:6-11, where we hear the promise that one day we will all bow to Jesus. Talk about what a sad day that will be for those who never believed that Jesus is who he said he is. They will bow down to Jesus, not because they love him, but because they have to finally admit he is God. What a great day, though, for all of us who do believe that Jesus is God's Son! We'll be able to love and worship him forever.

30. Did everyone in the Bible think Jesus was God?

Compare it. The probability of one person fulfilling even 48 major prophecies, according to Peter Stoner in *Science Speaks,* is 1 in 10 to the one-hundred-fifty-seventh power. That's the number 10 followed by 157 zeroes. The chance of someone fulfilling just eight prophecies is 1 in 10 to the seventeenth power. Share this picture with your child: "The chance that Jesus would fulfill just eight out of hundreds of prophecies is the same as the chance that you could find one marked silver dollar out of a pile of silver dollars in a pile two feet deep covering the whole state of Texas!"

31. Did Jesus actually die on the cross—or did he just faint?

Learn it. Talk with your family about the fact that if we get rid of the Resurrection, we get rid of Christianity. That's why so many non-Christians have tried to prove that Jesus never rose. No wonder Paul said we would be "the most miserable people in the world" if Christ were not alive (1 Corinthians 15:19). We would face all the trials, struggles, and problems of the Christian life—and then die with no hope of heaven. Thank God that he had a better plan!

32. Did Jesus really come back to life after he died on the cross?

Learn it. Help your child summarize the events of Christ's final week as described in the Gospels. Most children easily accept the resurrection as a fact. But if your child raises questions you can't answer, look for more in-depth answers in *More than a Carpenter* (Tyndale House Publishers, 1987) and *The New Evidence That Demands a Verdict* (Thomas Nelson, 1999).

33. Could Jesus' disciples have made up the story about Jesus coming back to life?

Learn it. Read in Matthew 28:11-15 about the efforts people made right from the start to disprove the resurrection. Talk with your child about why the leaders in the passage didn't want to believe that Jesus was alive. Explain that these leaders wanted people to follow them instead of Jesus.

34. How did Jesus come back to life?

Compare it. We don't have to understand exactly how God raised his Son, Jesus, from the dead to know that Jesus is truly alive. Most of us don't really know how cars work, yet we ride in them. Most of us don't have a clue how computers work, yet we use them and sometimes crash them! Even if we don't always understand the working of the Spirit, the amazing news is that the same power that raised Jesus from the dead will raise us to life in heaven (Romans 8:11)!

35. Is it okay to have Easter baskets and look for Easter eggs?

Ask it. Each family needs to make up its own mind about how to keep Christ at the center of the holidays. Ask your child, "How well do we do in remembering that Easter is about Jesus? Is there anything we want to do differently?" Read the verses from Matthew 28 again and talk about what a joyful message the angel had for the women. No matter how your family celebrates, it's important to be joyful over the Good News of the Resurrection.

QUESTIONS ABOUT THE HOLY SPIRIT

36. What's the Holy Spirit? Is he a ghost?

Learn it. Help your child understand that God as Father, Son, and Holy Spirit has always been around. Even at Creation, "the Spirit of God was hovering over" the formless Earth (Genesis 1:2). The Holy Spirit is present throughout the Old Testament (see, for example, Judges 3:10 and Micah 3:8). He is at the baptism of Jesus (Luke 3:22). Jesus said the Spirit would come to be with his disciples after he returned to the Father (John 14:15-17), a promise that was fulfilled at Pentecost (Acts 2:1-4).

37. How come I can't feel the Holy Spirit living in me?

Live it. Do you want to see more of the Holy Spirit's work in your family? Pray the following prayer from Ephesians 3:16-19. You may want to pray it aloud for your family members at least once a week. "I pray that from his glorious, unlimited resources [God] will give you mighty inner strength through his Holy Spirit. And I pray that Christ will be more and more at home in your hearts as you trust in him. May your roots go down deep into the soil of God's marvelous love. And may you have the power to understand, as all God's people should, how wide, how long, how high, and how deep his love really is...Then you will be filled with the fullness of life and power that comes from God."

QUESTION ABOUT THE DEVIL

38. Is the devil real?

Learn it. The devil is real, but he shouldn't be a fearful focus for your child. God's love and power are far better realities to fill your child's mind. If your child worries about the devil you can say, "Yes, the devil is real, and he is scary. But when we became Christians, we chased him out of our lives. He's not anywhere near as strong as God, so we can trust God to protect us."

QUESTIONS ABOUT THE BIBLE

39. How do some people know so much about God?

Live it. Talk about what you are doing each day to learn more about God. (Reading this book counts!) Pull out your family calendar: What might get in your way so you don't have time to learn to know God better? Choose one or two things each family member can do to learn more about God.

40. Why is the Bible so big?

Learn it. Help your child become familiar with the contents of the Bible. Show how it is split into the Old and New Testaments. Look at the names of the different books and start memorizing the names. You may also want to look up in a concordance or index the names of some favorite Bible characters. Show your child how to find the stories about these people in the Bible.

41. How is the Bible different from other books?

Share it. Talk with your child about how you have found the Bible to be the most important book you read. How is it different from other books on your shelf? How does it make a difference in your everyday life? Help your child understand that the Bible isn't a book we just listen to or read. It's a book with messages from God, who created us and wants us to learn the very best way to live.

42. Why did God put his words in a book?

Draw it. Find a map (or print one from the Web) that shows clearly how to get to your family's favorite restaurant, park, or vacation destination. Without showing your family members the map, have them draw their own map showing how to get to your special place. Point out—kindly!—that people who tried to follow those maps might get lost. Then show a real map and explain how it is like the Bible. "We can read what other people say about finding God. But God gave us the best directions in the Bible. He wanted us to have clear directions on how to find him and learn about him!"

43. How could God write a book?

Learn it. Explain that the Bible is different from any other Christian book written now or in the past. Before Jesus came to Earth, God chose people who loved and obeyed him to write down his very own message. After Jesus was born, God chose more people to write about his only Son, and how to believe in him and live for him. This completed what God wanted to tell us.

44. Who wrote down the words in the Bible?

Learn it. Focus on the way in which each Bible writer is special, pointing out that this is one of the Bible's coolest characteristics. To do this, read the different ways God spoke through the following writers about love. Through John: "God is love" (1 John 4:8); Paul: "Let love be your highest goal" (1 Corinthians 14:1); Jeremiah: "I have loved you, my people, with an everlasting love" (Jeremiah 31:3); Hosea: "Plant the good seeds of righteousness, and you will harvest a crop of my love" (Hosea 10:12); and Solomon: "A bowl of soup with someone you love is better than steak with someone you hate" (Proverbs 15:17).

45. How do we know the Bible is from God?

Act it. To make the point that we really need the Bible so that we can know God, hide your Bible behind your back. Then ask, "What would we know about God if he hadn't told us about himself in the Bible?" Some things we wouldn't know: How much God loves us; how God helped people like Noah, Abraham, Moses, Ruth, David, and Esther;

how Jesus was born, lived, died, and came back to life; how God wants us to love him and others; and so on. Next, say, "But we can thank God that he did give us a book that tells us what he is like—and how we can be friends with him."

46. The Bible is so old. How could it last so long?

Compare it. Talk about what might happen if you left a library book out in the rain. Explain that raindrops would ruin the book bit by bit until you owed a chunk of money for a new book. A baseball glove, however, would survive the rain—although it wouldn't be very soft. The people who protected the Bible were smart enough to write on the toughest materials they could find—things like leather and stone. And they didn't leave their Bibles out in the rain!

47. Are parts of the Bible make-believe, or is everything true?

Learn it. Have your child find in the Bible some of the stories of Jesus' miracles. Like Jesus feeding over 5,000 people from five loaves of bread and two fish (John 6:1-14). Or Jesus walking on water (Matthew 14:25). Or Jesus helping those who were blind to see (Matthew 9:30). Then turn to the book of Acts, in which Luke points out that the events recorded in the Bible "were not done in a corner" (Acts 26:26). Many people saw these events and agreed that they were true.

48. What will happen to people who don't obey the Bible?

Ask it. Talk over these questions with your child: "When have you been frustrated watching people do bad things—and seem to get away with it?" "What do you think will happen to people who do wrong? Will God stop them right away? Why or why not?" You can dig into the rest of Psalm 73, Lamentations 3:19-33, and the book of Habakkuk for more questions and answers.

49. Why is the Bible so hard to understand?

Live it. If your child has a tough time grasping the teachings of the Bible, shop for a version that is easier to understand. The Scripture quotations in this book are from the New Living Translation, unless otherwise identified. And for a good family devotional guide, look for the *One Year Book of Josh McDowell's Family Devotions 2* (Tyndale Kids, 2003). It is a product in the Beyond Belief campaign.

50. Why does the Bible have so many rules?

Learn it. Put these two important commands of Jesus at the front of your mind. Memorize them together with your family! And for the next several days, encourage one another by pointing out times when you see someone obeying one of these commands. If you see someone being disobedient, encourage that person to think of a way to change— to show love for God or love for a neighbor (which can include parents and siblings).

51. Are the Bible's rules old-fashioned?

Share it. Talk with your child about how the "old" rules of the Bible have helped you know how to do the right thing. How have you seen them work for your good?

52. Is the Bible always right?

Compare it. Explain that the Bible is like a big, sturdy trampoline. You can trust a trampoline to catch you no matter how high you jump. You can trust the Bible to be filled with solid truth from the Lord that will remain standing. It won't change or fall apart, no matter what. It's not like a rickety old chair that will break into pieces if you jump on it. You can always count on the Bible to have correct answers and help you do what's right

53. Why are there so many different kinds of Bibles?

Draw it. Here's an easy way to help your child see why we have so many Bibles. At the top of a sheet of paper, write "God is great!" (Psalm 70:4). Now fill up the paper with all the other ways you can say "great," from "super" and "neato" to "awesome," "funky," "phat," and "cool." As you decorate your sheet, ask, "What does each of these words say about God? Why would we pick one or another to say what he is like?" Explain that Bible translators choose words and phrases that will be easiest for their readers to understand. You can visit Wycliffe Bible Translators at www.wycliffe.org for resources to help your child understand why people of the world need the Bible in their own languages.

QUESTIONS ABOUT DIFFERENT RELIGIONS

54. Why do people from different religions sometimes fight?

Share it. Talk to your child about opportunities you have had to explain your faith to others—especially people who follow other faiths. How did you give reasons for your faith "in a gentle and respectful way"? How did you show love for the people you talked to?

55. Does my Muslim friend pray to the same God I do?

Live it. Talk with your child about friends or people you know who haven't trusted Christ because they follow a different faith. Make a plan together to lovingly help them learn about the one true God.

56. Do I have to tell people about Jesus?

Act it. Take time to talk and role-play situations likely to come up as your child shares her faith: What should she say? How should she say it? Who should she say it to? The best candidates for one-on-one sharing are people your child sees every day. And the first thing to share is your child's own experience of Christ's love—what Jesus has done for her!

57. Does it matter which God people believe in?

Ask it. Most children easily accept that God is real, and for most children that means the God of the Bible. But ask your child if she knows anyone who follows a different faith—or who doesn't seem to believe in God at all. Point out that many people say they believe in God but don't follow him, and many others commit their lives to other religions that don't believe Jesus is God's Son. Emphasize that our goal isn't to put down those people—or to stop being friends with them. Our job is to talk to them about Jesus' love for them. We want them to know Jesus can save all of us from sin. He gives joy and peace now. And his death on the cross makes it possible for us to live with God forever someday if we trust in him.

QUESTIONS ABOUT RIGHT AND WRONG

58. Can I decide for myself what's right and wrong?

Compare it. Making up our own minds about right and wrong is like being a sailor on the ocean who spins himself in a circle and points anywhere he pleases to decide which way is north. If he doesn't look up into the sky and chart his course by the North Star that God placed there, it won't be long before he's lost. If we ignore the fact that God alone gives us directions for the right way to live, we're going to do a lot of things that are wrong.

59. Why do we need rules?

Live it. Think together about some rules you have a tough time following. Write down these rules, and for each one, brainstorm three good reasons why that rule exists. How can obeying those rules help you find the "life in all its fullness" that God plans for you?

60. Does God punish me when I do wrong?

Share it. Explain that God created families and expects parents to lovingly discipline their children for wrong things they do. Talk about how you feel when your child does wrong. You forgive him for doing wrong—so you get over your anger and ask God to help you not to hold grudges. But you know your child still needs discipline so he or she will want to choose to do what's right the next time. You try to make sure good actions bring good results and bad actions bring bad results.

61. Why is it sometimes easier to do things that are wrong than to do what's right?

Act it. Often we feel like a huge tug-of-war is going on inside of us between the Holy Spirit and our sinful selves. Find a big rope or an old oversize beach towel and go outside for a game of tug-of-war. Then talk about this: "How does it feel when there's a battle between good and evil going on in us? How do we let the Holy Spirit win the tug-of-war?"

62. How does God help me choose to do the right thing?

Share it. How has trusting Jesus to meet your needs helped you make right choices? How has knowing him better changed what you wanted in life and how you went about getting it? Share one or two of these stories with your child. You may also want to discuss the difference between needs and wants. Explain that as we learn to know Jesus better, we start looking at things the way he does. So what we want does change to become what we really need.

63. Why do I sometimes get in trouble for doing the right thing?

Act it. Christian kids can run into trouble not just with adult authorities but with peers. Ask your child if an adult has ever mistakenly accused her of doing wrong—or if another kid has made fun of her for something she said or did because she was trying to follow Jesus. Then role-play how your child can respond to being wrongly accused—or to being picked on for being a believer.

64. Why do some Christians not act like Christians?

Live it. Help your child name some actions that would be hypocritical for a Christian and wouldn't honor Jesus Christ. Then pray for your family, your church, your pastor, and other Christian leaders—that all believers would stay away from hypocritical actions and "live in a way that brings honor to the Good News of Christ" (Philippians 1:27 NCV).

QUESTIONS ABOUT THE FUTURE

65. Does God know what my life will be like when I grow up?

Learn it. Discuss with your child the fact that God's plan for each of us has two parts. The first is God's clear will for everyone—his "universal will." The second is God's will for each individual—his "specific will." God's universal will is what we learn from God's commands and principles in the Bible. It's where all Christians need to start when we want to do God's will—and it's the most basic place for children to start as they learn to be disciples. Once we begin to obey God's commands for everyone, we're in the right place to find God's will for us as individuals. God reveals this specific part of his plan step-by-step through the Bible, prayer, things that happen, and wise advice from other Christians.

66. Does God care what job I have when I grow up?

Share it. Share with your child how you see God's plan for you at work in how you spend your adult life. Talk about the gifts and abilities God has given you to help you do your job. Help your child identify some gifts and abilities that may help her know what work God wants her to do someday.

67. Will God tell me what will happen in my future?

Draw it. Have your child draw a picture entitled "My Future Is in God's Hands." Give him free rein to draw whatever he thinks his future might look like. Ask your child to tell you about each part of the picture. Then pray for God's wisdom as you and your child trust God to direct every path.

68. Why does God let bad things happen to me sometimes?

Live it. Explain that the bad things, big or small, that happen to us daily cause feelings of sadness. Read Romans 12:15 together: "When others are happy, be happy with them. If they are sad, share their sorrow." Then pray for someone who is feeling sad—pray that God would show you how to comfort that person. Remind your child that bad things will happen on this Earth, but in heaven there will be no more sadness.

69. Can God make bad things turn out okay?

Live it. Do you know anyone who is facing a difficult time right now? Make a plan as a family to show that person God's wonderful love and care.

QUESTIONS ABOUT CHURCH

70. Why do we go to church?

Compare it. God put us together in the church to keep our friendship with him warm and bright. Explain to your child that the church is like a roaring campfire. A coal kept in the center of the flame will glow all night. But a coal pushed off to the side goes out and its warmth quickly fades. The people in a church family need to stay together just like those coals need to stick close together.

71. Why does church last so long?

Learn it. Talk with your child about what's exciting at church. How do the songs, the Bible lessons, the prayers, the service projects, and so on, help each of you love Jesus more? Every activity your family participates in at church should take you and your children beyond belief. It should take you from a mere familiarity with the truths of the Christian faith into a life-changing love relationship with God and your fellow believers. If you aren't confident that you or your children are being led step-by-step into a real, lifelong friendship with Jesus, you can be part of a revolution in your church. Visit www.unshakabletruth.com to learn how.

72. My friend doesn't go to church—what should I do?

Live it. Who in your child's world needs to meet Jesus—maybe in a deep way, maybe for the first time? What can you do as a family to help that friend connect with Jesus? You might want to plan some activities at your house in which your child invites both Christian and non-Christian friends. Perhaps you can offer to pick up a neighboring child for Sunday school. Or your child could invite a friend to an after-school Bible club.

QUESTIONS ABOUT DEATH AND HEAVEN

73. Why did my grandma die when the Bible says that Christians will live forever?

Share it. Explain to your child how the death of a Christian close to you brought you a mixture of sadness and joy—sadness that your loved one was physically gone, but joy that he or she will live forever with Jesus. Let your child express her own feelings related to the loss of a life. It could be a church friend, a neighbor, or a relative.

74. What will I look like in heaven?

Compare it. Find something around your home that needs fixing and set it in front of your child. Getting a new body in heaven, you can explain, is like completely remaking that broken object. If you could make all new parts—and fashion them so they would last forever—then you would have something like our new heavenly bodies. The broken object would be the same—but better than ever!

75. Will everybody go to heaven?

The people in Matthew 24 thought that Jesus was slow about coming back to Earth (verses 36-44). But any delay in his return is time for more people to repent. God wants all people to turn away from their sins and follow him. Act out the word *repent* by having your child walk away from you, then turn around and walk back to you. Explain, "That's what it means to repent. When you sin, it's like walking away from God. Then God commands you to turn around—to leave your sinful beliefs and actions and come back to him, believing and acting the way he wants you to. That's what God wants all of us to do!" A moving end to this exercise would be to exchange places and act out your own repentance by coming back to your child.

76. How long will we be in heaven?

Compare it. Think together of the best moments you have had as a family. Explain, "That's just a little taste of what heaven might be like. What makes heaven even better is that God himself will be there, and he will make it a place we will enjoy being forever and ever." Then read Revelation 21:3-4: "I heard a loud shout from the throne, saying, 'Look, the home of God is now among his people! He will live with them, and they will be his people. God himself will be with them. He will remove all of their sorrows, and there will be no more death or sorrow or crying or pain. For the old world and its evils are gone forever.'" Heaven isn't just about eternal life. It's about eternal love and happiness!

77. How do I know I'm going to heaven?

Draw it. Explain that Jesus has sent each of us an invitation to heaven. Say, "We are invited to believe in Jesus and trust him to give us eternal life. Going to live with Jesus in heaven forever will be like going to a party that never ends!" Have your child choose some words from John 14:6 or John 5:24 to design and decorate an invitation to God's eternal home.

index of Bible Verses

Genesis 1:31 Question 1

Exodus 34:27 Question 44

2 Samuel 7:22 Question 57

Psalm 19:7, 11 Question 4

Psalm 19:8 Question 42

Psalm 32:2-3 Question 3

Psalm 33:4-5 Question 58

Psalm 62:8 Question 23

Psalm 73:3, 17-18 Question 48

Psalm 86:5, 10 Question 15

Psalm 100:3 Question 14

Psalm 103:12 Question 13

Psalm 111:7-8 Question 52

Psalm 119:105 Question 49

Psalm 119:105-106 Question 59

Psalm 119:152 Question 51

Psalm 139:1 Question 19

Proverbs 3:5-6 Question 67

Proverbs 4:18-19 Question 9

Proverbs 16:9 Question 65

Isaiah 53:5 Question 10

Habakkuk 1:13 Question 5

Matthew 22:37-39 Question 50

Matthew 24:35 Question 53

Matthew 26:59-60 Question 25

Matthew 28:5-6 Question 35

Matthew 28:19-20 Question 56

Mark 1:35 Question 17

Luke 2:52 Question 28

John 1:11-12 Question 30

John 1:18 Question 2

John 5:24 Question 73

John 10:32-33 Question 29

John 14:6 Question 77

John 14:13-14 Question 24

John 14:16-17 Question 36

John 15:15 Question 39

John 20:30-31 Question 40

John 21:24 Question 33

Romans 1:4 Question 34

Romans 3:22 Question 12

Romans 3:25 Question 7

Romans 5:8 Question 16

Romans 6:23 Question 6

Romans 8:11 Question 31

Romans 8:28-29 Question 69

Romans 8:38 Question 20

Romans 12:5 Question 70

Romans 12:14, 17 Question 63

1 Corinthians 10:11 Question 47

1 Corinthians 15:3-4 Question 32

1 Corinthians 15:42, 44 Question 74

Galatians 4:7 Question 8

Galatians 5:16 Question 61

Galatians 5:22-23 Question 37

Ephesians 3:17 Question 27

Philippians 1:27 Question 64

Colossians 3:23 Question 66

1 Thessalonians 4:17 Question 76

1 Timothy 2:5-6 Question 55

2 Timothy 3:15 Question 41

2 Timothy 3:16 Question 45

Hebrews 4:15-16 Question 26

Hebrews 10:25 Question 71

Hebrews 12:5-6 Question 60

James 4:7-8 Question 38

1 Peter 1:6-7 Question 68

1 Peter 1:17 Question 21

1 Peter 1:18-19 Question 18

1 Peter 1:24-25 Question 46

1 Peter 2:9-10 Question 72

1 Peter 3:15-16 Question 54

1 Peter 5:7 Question 22

2 Peter 1:3 Question 62

2 Peter 3:9 Question 75

2 Peter 1:20-21 Question 43

1 John 1:8-9 Question 11

Index of Topics by Question Number

Bible 39–53

Church 70–72

Death and heaven 73–77

Devil 38

Forgiveness 10–13

Future 65–69

God 1–2

God's love 14–21

Holy Spirit 36–37

Jesus 25–35

Prayer 22–24

Religions 54–57

Right and wrong 58–64

Sin 3–9

Resources from Josh and Sean McDowell

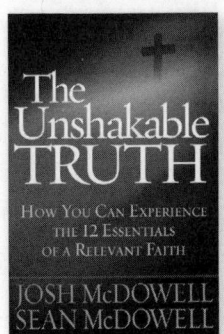

The Unshakable Truth™
How You Can Experience the 12 Essentials
of a Relevant Faith
Josh and Sean McDowell

As a Christian, you may feel unsure about what you believe and why. Maybe you wonder if your faith is even meaningful and credible.

Unpacking 12 biblical truths that define the core of Christian belief and Christianity's reason for existence, this comprehensive yet easy-to-understand handbook helps you discover

- the foundational truths about God, his Word, sin, Christ, the Trinity, the church, and six more that form the bedrock of Christian faith

- how you can live out these truths in relationship with God and others

- ways to pass each truth on to your family and the world around you

Biblically grounded, spiritually challenging, and full of practical examples and real-life stories, *The Unshakable Truth* is a resource applicable to every aspect of everyday life.

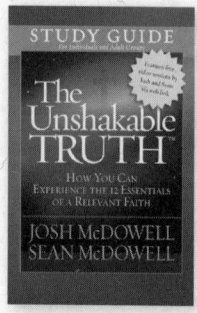

The Unshakable Truth™ Study Guide

Josh and Sean McDowell

This study guide offers you—or you and your group—a *relational experience* to discover...

- 12 foundational truths of Christianity—in sessions about God, his Word, the Trinity, Christ's atonement, his resurrection, his return, the church, and five more

- "Truth Encounter" exercises to actually help you live out these key truths

- "TruthTalk" assignments on ways to share the essentials of the faith with your family and others

Through twelve 15-minute Web-link videos, Josh and Sean McDowell draw on their own father-son legacy of faith to help you feel adequate to impart what you believe with confidence. *Includes instructions for group leaders.*

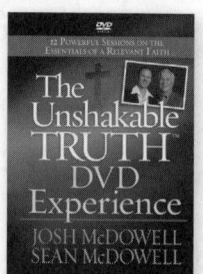

The Unshakable Truth™ DVD Experience
12 Powerful Sessions on the Essentials of a Relevant Faith
Josh and Sean McDowell

What do I believe, and why do I believe it? How is it relevant to my life? How do I live it out?

If you're asking yourself questions like these, you're not alone. In 12 quick, easy-to-grasp video sessions based on their book *The Unshakable Truth*, Josh and Sean McDowell give a solid introduction to the foundations of the faith.

Josh and Sean outline 12 key truths with clear explanations, compelling discussions, and provocative "on-the-street" interviews. And uniquely, they explain these truths *relationally*, showing you how living them out changes you and affects family and friends—everyone you encounter. *Helpful leader's directions included.*

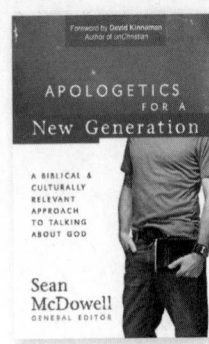

Apologetics for a New Generation
A Biblical and Culturally Relevant Approach to Talking About God
Sean McDowell

This generation's faith is constantly under attack from the secular media, skeptical teachers, and unbelieving peers. You may wonder, *How can I help?*

Working with young adults every day, Sean McDowell understands their situation and shares your concern. His first-rate team of contributors shows how you can help members of the new generation plant their feet firmly on the truth. Find out how you can walk them through the process of...

- formulating a biblical worldview and applying scriptural principles to everyday issues

- articulating their questions and addressing their doubts in a safe environment

- becoming confident in their faith and effective in their witness

More Family Resources from Harvest House

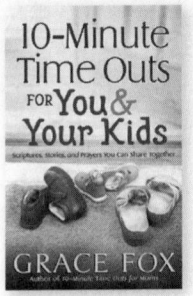

10-Minute Time Outs for You and Your Kids
Scripture, Stories, and Prayers You Can Share Together
Grace Fox

These brief devotions pack excitement and encouragement in a "treasure hunt" through the Bible. In ten minutes a day, you'll

- *read the clue*—share a key verse for the day
- *discover the treasure*—hear a brief story and the truth it portrays
- *share the wealth*—offer a Scripture-based prayer and discuss a question or do the suggested activity
- *hide a jewel*—memorize a verse that reinforces the day's theme

Your family can become rich—filled with the truth about who God is and how He wants His children to live.

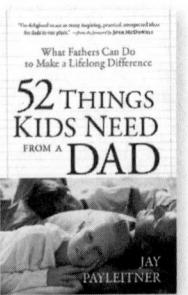

52 Things Kids Need from a Dad
What Fathers Can Do to Make a Lifelong Difference
Jay Payleitner

> "I'm delighted to see so many inspiring, practical, unexpected ideas for dads in one place."
> JOSH MCDOWELL

Good news—you are already the perfect dad for your kids! Still, you know you can grow. In these pages, Jay Payleitner, veteran radio producer and dad of five, offers a bounty of inspiring and unexpected insights:

- *straightforward rules*: "carry photos of your kids," "dad tucks in," and "kiss your wife in the kitchen"
- *candid advice that may be tough to hear*: "get right with your own dad," "throw out your porn," and "surrender control of the TV remote"
- *weird topics that at first seem absurd*: "buy Peeps," "spin a bucket over your head" and "rent a dolphin"

Surely, God—our heavenly Father—designed fatherhood to be a joy, a blessing, and a blast!

The Ultimate Bible Quiz Book

Douglas Jacoby

- Jesus never wrote a book. True or false?

- Who was Abraham's second son?

- What is another name for the Promised Land?

These intriguing Bible quizzes will provide hours of fun whether you try them alone or enjoy them with your family or friends. Each is one page long, with answers on the back of the page. Questions range from simple to advanced and from commonsense to mind-bending, so whether you're a longtime Bible reader or are just getting started, jump in, test your knowledge, and learn as you go!

Amazing Bible Word Searches for Kids

Richard and Ruth Spiering

These amazing word search puzzles are exciting to do, and you get to learn great Bible facts at the same time. You'll discover...

- the unusual way the apostle Paul met Jesus

- what salvation, faith, and grace mean

- what mammals, birds, and insects lived in Bible lands

- what equipment soldiers used when fighting their enemies

- what musical instruments were used in Bible times

And as an extra challenge, many of these word searches have hidden messages for you to discover. So sharpen your pencil and get started today. *Perfect for vacations, car rides, plane trips, church camps, and church-related activities.*